PRIESTLY
FATHERHOOD

PRIESTLY

Treasure in Earthen Vessels

FATHERHOOD

Jacques Philippe

 Scepter

While every effort has been made to obtain existing accepted English translations, some quotes have been translated by Scepter Publishers when no accepted English equivalent has been found.

Published by Scepter Publishers, Inc.
info@scepterpublishers.org
www.scepterpublishers.org
800-322-8773
New York

Cover and page design by Rose Design
Translation from French by Neal Carter

Library of Congress Control Number: 2020947773
ISBN: 978-1-59417-417-9 (pbk.)
ISBN: 978-1-59417-418-6 (eBook)

Printed in the United States of America

Contents

∿

PART TWO / 61

A PROFOUND TRANSFORMATION OF HEART

Part Three / 133

A Tangible Reality

Introduction

The topic of priestly spiritual fatherhood is an important one today. It is a delicate topic, particularly in light of the sad revelation of the behavior of some priests which is in total contradiction with true fatherhood.

There is nonetheless an enormous need in our world for people who are authentic reflections of divine fatherhood. Not that it's their exclusive domain, but I think that it forms an essential part of the priestly vocation.

For the priest himself, experiencing the unfolding of a true fatherhood in the exercise of his ministry is a real grace; it gives his priesthood a quite invigorating depth and beauty.

Through this little book, I would like to encourage my brother priests, who often have a pressing need for encouragement, and to help them believe in the fruitfulness—the fertility—and the beauty of their vocations. Even if it's a difficult, demanding reality, fatherhood is also a source of great joy. There is nothing more beautiful than to give life, and so much more so when this life is eternal life, the very life of God.

My book is addressed especially to priests, but I think that all people who are called to exercise a certain form of paternity (the fathers of a family, spiritual fathers, educators, people in positions of authority . . .) could find some useful elucidation on how to live their responsibilities fairly.

PART ONE

— ✤ —

Fatherhood, a Difficult but Essential Reality

Precautions on Language

Treating this topic requires caution for many reasons.

There is a warning Jesus gives in the Gospel of Matthew: *"Call no man your father on earth, for you have one Father, who is in heaven"* (Mt 23:9).

Jesus teaches us through these words that there is really only one fatherhood—that of God—and that all human fatherhood, especially the priest's, only makes sense in the measure of how much it is at the service of divine paternity, in which human fatherhood finds its origin and its final end: helping men and women be sons and daughters of God. Priestly fatherhood is not something that the priest possesses in himself, but a humble service of the only essential paternity, which is God's. The priest's own person is in no way the source or the goal of the relationship that he encourages as a priest with those entrusted to him in his ministry. It's not about making them his own children but making them the children of the heavenly Father.

Note also that while Scripture and the Tradition both speak of priestly ministry, the preferred image for describing this ministry is not the image of a father, which is actually used quite rarely, but rather the image of a shepherd. The priest is a good shepherd who takes care of his sheep, and who would even go so far as to give his own life for them. The sacramental grace of the priest is first of all the grace to be established, as was the good shepherd, Christ. Fatherhood can only come after, building on the base of pastoral charity. In a certain sense, fatherhood is not something that the priest can attain directly. He must first strive to be a good shepherd. If he really is, the grace of fatherhood can then be given to him.

Another observation is that the grace of the priesthood is above all a grace to be like Christ, who is not a father, but is the Son. If it's legitimate to speak of priestly paternity (and I think it is), this paternity cannot be founded on anything other than participation in the sonship of Jesus with his Father.

What justifies the language of paternity when speaking of the priesthood are Jesus' words to Philip in the Gospel of John: "He who has seen me has seen the Father" (Jn 14:9). Jesus is the Son, but in living this sonship fully, he reveals it in a new way, making God's fatherhood visible: the infinite, tender, merciful love of the Father for all his children. In the same way, if a priest lets himself be fashioned after Christ, he makes the face and love of the Father visible.

Even more so than theological reflection, what legitimizes the language of paternity is the witness, throughout the history of the Church, of so many holy bishops and priests through whom God's paternity is manifested for the good of all. I'm thinking particularly of all the bishop saints from history, from St. Paul to St. Francis de Sales to Pope St. John Paul II. I'm also thinking of so many holy and good priests who were pastors, educators, or missionaries, full of kindness and care for their flocks, of whom we could make a list longer than this book, without even counting those that history hasn't recorded. They wouldn't have claimed the title "Father" and would have felt unworthy, but the Christian people have recognized them as father figures and so used the name.

Some years ago, while I was visiting an exhibit on St. John Bosco at the house where he started his youth work in the Valdocco neighborhood of Turin, I was touched by a photograph showing him among a group of young people who were all pressing in on him, like children surrounding their father. It was an overwhelming image of true paternity and of affection, an image of the recognition of these young people for the man who pulled them out of misery and ignorance.

Without a doubt, the greatest joys in a priest's life are these moments when he experiences true fatherhood.

The priestly ministry is often difficult, sometimes lived through the "monotony of sacrifice" (according to The Little Flower, St. Thérèse of Lisieux's, expression) more than in endless enthusiasm. The priest's fate is often a daily life led through a dryness of faith. Nonetheless, if we are faithful to our mission, there are moments of grace where we feel our hearts filled up with a deep love, an immense tenderness for the people that God entrusts to us; we feel a paternal, even almost maternal, love for them. This can well up during an encounter with young people, in preaching to a crowd, in individual contact with a suffering person, in the context of confession. . . . At these times we feel our hearts fill up with a love that is greater than ourselves, a love that cannot find its source in our hearts alone. We feel a tenderness, a much greater compassion, stronger and purer than our natural capabilities could attain. This is God who is coming to love through us, who gives us the grace to feel his kindness and pity for his children. We receive in our earthly hearts the same sentiments of the very heart of Jesus, just as described in the Gospels, for example in Matthew: "When he saw the crowds, he had compassion for them, because they were harassed and helpless, like sheep without a shepherd" (Mt 9:36).

Sometimes we are seized with compassion in the same way, even moved to tears, and we want to be able to take every one of these people into our arms to communicate all the tenderness and consolation of God!

These are the times when the priest is happy to be a priest, when he feels that he is able to love, in spite of his human poverty and limits, with a love that God himself has for his children.

True fatherhood shows itself little by little in those who let themselves be fashioned after Christ in their priestly lives. It is not something that we can claim for ourselves or impose on others: "I am a priest, therefore from now on you must accept me as your father!" This doesn't work, especially today. Fatherhood is something difficult and demanding, which requires a continuous path of conversion through little adjustments and proper orientation toward a pure, disinterested love. We can't give God's people false currency—they figure it out really fast. We only become a father progressively, particularly through the emptying of self.

Being a priest and representing God is not a glorious title, but an enormous responsibility. How many people have left the Church because they were hurt by the attitude of certain priests?

1

A Priestly Pentecost

I think that the Lord is planning a priestly renewal, and that all the recent, painful revelations on the subject of the sin of some priests are as much an invitation to a purification and a deep renewal of the priesthood as they are signs of the work of the Holy Spirit, who will make the priesthood beautiful again. I'd like to quote a few lines from a book that was published recently[1] reporting Jesus' words to a Benedictine monk. He was called to consecrate his life to praying for the renewal of the priesthood and founded a monastery in Ireland to this goal's end. These words were communicated to him in October 2007.

> Today, I think that it was during the Glorious Mysteries of the Rosary, the Lord spoke to me of a sacerdotal (priestly) Pentecost, of a grace obtained

---

1. A Benedictine Monk, *In Sinu Jesu: When Heart Speaks to Heart— The Journal of a Priest at Prayer*, (Brooklyn, NY: Angelico Press, 2016), 22 [French edition].

through the intercession of the Virgin Mary for all the priests of the Church. To all [priests] will be offered the grace of a new outpouring of the Holy Spirit to purify the priesthood of the impurities that have disfigured it, and to restore to the priesthood a brightness of holiness such as the Church has never had since the time of the Apostles.

Other passages from this book echo the same sentiment and insist upon the fact of this priestly renewal, this purification and healing of hearts, coming particularly from Eucharistic Adoration by priests (and also by the faithful) and a filial love for the Virgin Mary.[2]

The author affirms that, thanks to this renewed priesthood, the Lord will give the world priests whose ministry will be a source of comfort and healing for much of the suffering caused by the absence of true fathers.

I completely share this conviction. God cannot abandon his Church or his priests, and, according to St. Paul's words, "where sin increased, grace abounded all the more" (Rom 5:20).

---

2. Benedictine Monk, in particular, p. 159–160 and 197–199.

2

The Urgent Need for Fatherhood

As we all know, there is a crisis of fatherhood today. Fatherhood is often invalidated, all paternity or authority being suspected of abuse or of being overbearing. The image of the father in modern culture is often pale and oblivious, even to the point of being made a caricature, whereas the mother is seen as capable and strong. Men who present a positive image of paternity are lacking in modern society. Fathers of families don't always play the role that they should assume, and they no longer know very well how to act. Paternity is in crisis in the Church; it is also suffering in the world of education and schools. Not to mention politics, where politicians more often give the impression of being argumentative children than people who may be given the chance one day to be recognized as the "father of the nation," like some of their predecessors. There is also a crisis of masculinity, which is inevitable, really, given that true virility, in the end, can't be accomplished without a certain form of paternity.

In spite of this context—or rather because of this context—the need for true paternity has never been greater than it is today. We are in a world of orphans, and so many people are disoriented and suffering because they haven't had the chance of meeting someone in their lives who was a true father.

I notice it particularly in my own ministry. I encounter a great number of people, and I must say that I am hit by the realization of how desperate is the need for paternity. Whether it be children, young adults, couples, adults, or old grandmothers, all have this need for a father figure. It's not always expressed outright because of fear or pride, which discourages acknowledging it, but it exists in all without exception. In my ministry, I've had important businessmen in front of me, people at the head of big enterprises, who nevertheless come up after a conference to ask for a big hug, at the point of tears when I embrace them.

Every man and woman needs to find a father on whom they can rely and by whom they are recognized, loved, and encouraged. This father is, of course, above all, the Father in Heaven; but each time that a man or woman finds him- or herself faced with someone who, by their manner of being, represents an authentic image of God's paternity, it's a great gift.

3

⁓

Suffering Caused by the Absence of a Father

The absence of a father figure (that of God himself, but also those who, in one way or another, are human versions of divine paternity) causes painful consequences in people's lives. I don't want to give an exhaustive list here, but will only mention four points.

1. Without Fatherhood, There Is a Transmission Problem

The role of a father is to inscribe a child into a lineage, giving access to a heritage, a heritage that the child must later transmit to others. It's a question of transmission, and we know how difficult it is already today to transmit from one generation to the next everything that makes up the richness and beauty of existence: the human and spiritual virtues, the culture, the traditions belonging to a country, and more. The lack of a paternal role makes this transmission more difficult, of course. We notice that this shortcoming produces a certain type of personality: the individual who has no awareness of what is owed to those who came before, who has no sense of responsibility toward those who will come after. Without gratitude for the past, and without responsibility to others for the future, that person will be content to profit from life to the maximum in a selfish and individualistic manner. This type of attitude is not rare today.

2. Without Fatherhood, There Is No Mercy

The modern world believed it was good to proclaim the death of God. It acceded to the great lie of atheism: by his laws and commandments, God prevents man from being free; we must, therefore, get rid of him, and then the human person will finally be free and happy, set free from constraints and guilt! Even though this lie has led to millions of deaths, the temptation both to make God (and all forms of paternity) the enemy of human freedom, and to consider all verticality as oppression, still persists.

But things aren't as simple as atheism supposes. If there is no God, there is no forgiveness or mercy.

We all like the parable of the Prodigal Son in the Gospel of St. Luke (see Lk 15), which gives us a marvelous view of divine paternity. We recognize the story of the younger of the two brothers, who claimed his inheritance and went off to a foreign land. After everything was spent in a life of disorder, he found himself watching over pigs (not particularly a success story for a young man from a Jewish family!), dying of hunger, and envying the food given to the swine. The situation led him to self-reflection and he resolved to return to his father's house, where even the servants were fed abundantly. He prepared his little arrival speech: "Father, I have sinned against Heaven and before you; I am no longer worthy to be called your son; treat me like one of your hired hands."

We all know the unexpected ending of this story: the father sees his son arriving from afar and, seized with pity for him, runs to cover him with kisses! And without giving him time for the prepared speech, the father gives orders to his servants: *Quickly* bring him suitable clothing (not just any clothing, but *the most beautiful*), put a ring on his finger (a sign of regained dignity), put sandals on his feet, and prepare for him a big party, complete with fat veal, music, and dancing.

Let's take up the same story again, but this time let's eliminate the father figure. When the son comes back to the house, there is nobody . . . the house is empty, hopelessly empty, abandoned. Only the wind beats against the doors and windows.

There is nobody to welcome him, no one to pardon him, no one to love him. No one to tell him, "In spite of what you've done, in spite of your errors and your sin, you remain my well-loved son, you can regain your full dignity, you have a place here, and you can be free and happy in the house of your father, the house which is also your house! *Everything I have is yours!*"

I think that we cannot forgive ourselves for the sins we've committed (and we've all committed sin!). We cannot absolve ourselves of our errors, even with an army of psychologists trying to take away our guilt. I have nothing against psychologists—quite the contrary, they often do excellent work—but they cannot forgive sins.

We need to receive the absolution of someone bigger than ourselves. We need the words of Another, words of authority, the words of the Heavenly Father, in order to be truly set free from faults and reconciled with ourselves.

These considerations make us measure the immense grace that is given to the priest in being able to pronounce the words of absolution, even though they are said in passing, to those who come to confess to him. He knows that, in spite of his personal limits, when he tells someone, "I absolve you from your sins," the words he pronounces are not simply human words, but rather, that they have the very authority of Holy Scripture. They have the power to free the sinner from the evil of which he is culpable, restore his dignity, and give him freedom and peace. What a joy to be able to be such an instrument of God's mercy! Giving priestly forgiveness is perhaps the closest participation in God's fatherhood.

We know that in the Old Testament, the use of the word "Father" when referring to God is rather infrequent, in order to avoid confusing God's paternity with the male pagan gods who participated in sexual procreation. In other words, the term "Father" is used less in the context of creation than in the context of redemption, an invocation of God's mercy in saving his people. One of the most beautiful passages from the Old Testament evoking God as father is found in chapters 63 and 64 of the prophet Isaiah, the following passage, in particular:

> We have all become like one who is unclean, and all our righteous deeds are like a polluted garment. We all fade like a leaf, and our iniquities, like the wind, take us away. There is no one who calls on thy name, that bestirs himself to take hold of thee; for thou hast hid thy face from us, and hast delivered us into the hand of our iniquities. Yet, O Lord, thou art our Father; we are the clay, and thou art our potter; we are all the work of thy hand. Be not exceedingly

angry, O Lord, and remember not iniquity forever.
Behold, consider, we are all thy people. (Is 64:6–9)

Without the presence of the merciful Father, we are
delivered up to our faults, without any possible remedy.
There would be no forgiveness of error or sin. No place
for weakness, frailty, or failure, all of which are nonetheless a part of our lives.

We would be, in a way, condemned to succeed at
life, something that really would be terrible. It would
mean putting a terrible weight on our shoulders, an
obligation to be superhuman, going from success to success without any possibility of failure. Maybe I'm exag-
gerating a bit in saying this, but this is the sense that our
society has tended towards, lacking more and more pity
for human faults.

Today we're living through the paradox of a society
that, on one hand, is very lax and permissive, and on
the other hand, without mercy for those who make mistakes! In the Kingdom of God, it is exactly the reverse:
there are both strong requirements that show us the cor-
rect path for life, as well as great mercy that offers the
continuous possibility of renewal in case of error.[1]

---

1. A beautiful mediation on the parable of the Prodigal Son (as well as
on the famous Rembrandt painting), which is also a profound reflection
on fatherhood, is Henri Nouwen's book, *The Return of the Prodigal Son.*

3. Without Fatherhood, Freedom Becomes Too Burdensome

Another consequence of putting God aside and of rejecting all forms of paternity is that the question of freedom, which is joined to responsibility, becomes very problematic.

Without reference to God, we run the strong risk of becoming irresponsible. "If God does not exist, everything is permitted!" Ivan Karamazov affirms in Dostoyevsky's novel, *The Brothers Karamazov*. A society without fathers runs the risk of becoming a world of irresponsible people; we must take note that our culture is creating greater and greater narcissists, that is to say, people who follow no other law than pleasure, no other rules than satisfying their desires.

But there is also the opposite problem in society: not an absence, but a sort of excess of responsibility. I think that there is a real question here: our society is becoming more and more free, social norms are imposed less and less, there is an increasing amount of poor conduct considered acceptable, and the array of possible unrestricted human choices is ever larger. Let's take the example of sexuality. Because of evolving viewpoints on the matter, and because of technical advancements regarding sexuality, all leading to the diffusion of theories on gender, the possible choices in this domain have expanded greatly, in terms of sexual conduct, family composition, procreation, and the like. We have arrived at the point where a little boy or girl risks being led one day to the question: do I remain as I am or shall I change my sex? A couple I know was sadly confronted with this exact situation: their 17-year-old daughter adamantly demanded to change her sex!

We have here the paradox of immense freedom on one side, but on the other side the refusal of God, a refusal of any objective truth. Faced with the latter the person is ultimately alone in deciding, each person being charged with constructing his or her own truth and with being the judge of the value of his or her decisions.[2] An enormous freedom weighs on the shoulders of the individual, without anyone to help discern what would be good among possible decisions both for the individual and for others. This is one of the roles of the father figure, not to alienate or crush human freedom, but to support it and orient it in discerning choices. In the absence of this support and orientation, freedom

---

2. This is one of the paradoxes of the current world. In the political or public sphere, we are attentive in carefully distinguishing the executive, legislative, and judicial powers necessary for the healthy functioning of society. On the other hand, in the private sphere, because of individualism and relativism, we are more and more led to be our own legislator (each of us creating our own moral code) and our own judge. It's a situation that is highly unhealthy and untenable in the long run.

risks becoming folly because it has no compass, and it becomes too heavy a load for human shoulders.

When we leave the Father's house, there can be a kind of intoxication of freedom. "Finally, I can do whatever I want!" But there is a strong risk of going from this to disillusion, and even anguish, under the weight of a freedom that becomes too heavy to carry.

I am persuaded that a kind of anxiety is present in our world, particularly for youth at the cusp of adult life, whose principle cause is that they dispose of great latitude, of so many possible choices, but without having anyone near them, a father figure, to help them exercise this freedom. The absence or the abdication of true fathers, and their replacement with false prophets of the libertarian revolution, risks leading young adults to an insufferable anguish.

4. Without Fatherhood, No Brotherhood is Possible

The French Republic adopted the slogan "Liberty, Equality, Fraternity" as its motto. A Christian must subscribe to this motto too, only he or she would be wise to remark that it is very difficult to establish a true brotherhood among all without recognition of the ineffable fatherhood of God. (Just as without reference to God, it's hard to see what remains of freedom and equality!)

When we realize that we have a common Father, it's easier to welcome one another as siblings, recognizing our equality and deep dignity, assuming the duties and responsibilities that we have toward each other. In the absence of a father, how do we recognize our brothers and sisters, sons and daughters of the same family, people of the same origin and the same dignity? What foundation is there to brotherhood?

Holy Scripture does not have an idealistic or romantic vision of brotherhood. If Psalm 133 proclaims "Behold, how good and pleasant it is when brothers dwell in unity!" (verse 1), the Bible shows at the same time the realization that true brotherhood is very difficult. Look at the relationships between Cain and Abel, Jacob and Esau, Joseph and his brothers. Such rivalries and conflicts! But there is always the possibility of resolving these. Joseph forgives and his brothers are reconciled.

The reality of the unique divine paternity, the acceptance of the Father's grace and mercy in the Son, always opens a path of reconciliation and pardon. "For as many of you as were baptized into Christ have put on Christ. There is neither Jew nor Greek, there is neither slave nor free, there is neither male nor female; for you are all one in Christ Jesus," according to Paul's beautiful words (Gal 3:27–28).

When God and the mystery of his paternity are refused, the unity of the human family becomes much more difficult. We can clearly see, through the evolution of today's society, how the rejection of God—of all fatherhood, of a truth that is authoritative for all—consequently makes relationships between persons more and more filled with conflict. What reigns in the place of unity is rivalry, a permanent competition that prevails everywhere. Man and woman become enemies of one another, social fabric breaks down, mistrust and violence are increasingly introduced into the relationships between people and different social groups.

We have just taken a look at the difficulties and suffering that an absence of fatherhood brings forth. All of that shouldn't discourage us, though. We must see it as a strong invitation to return to God, "from whom every family in heaven and on earth is named" (Eph 3:15).

Where human fatherhood is absent or lacking, as in the lives of many people, divine fatherhood can provide a source of renewal and healing. It is urgent to proclaim the gospel, letting every person discover the gentle and powerful fatherhood of God, discover Christ as the image and instrument of the Father's mercy, receive the outpouring of the Holy Spirit that makes us cry out "Abba! Father!" that witnesses "with our spirit that we are children of God" (Rm 8:15–16). Each and every person must hear the voice of the Father saying, as he did to Jesus, "Thou art my beloved Son; with thee I am well pleased" (Mk 1:11).

We must also insistently beg God that he bring up people in society and in the Church, especially priests, who are authentic reflections of God's fatherhood.

4

The Gift of Fatherhood

Let's move on to take a positive look at things now, by attempting to remind ourselves in a few words what a gift true fatherhood can be for the person who encounters it and experiences it.

The father helps his child find his or her true identity. In the Bible, the father gives the child its name. The name is not just a label, a word to be called by, but it represents a deep identity, the mission of the person.

The father confirms the child's identity, assuring them that they have the right to exist, the right to be whoever they are. "Thou art my beloved Son; with thee I am well pleased" (Mk 1:11). He allows the child to realize the deep truth of his or her being. Feeling welcomed and fully loved, the son or daughter perceives that they have the right to live according to their proper identity, the freedom to be themselves, to develop the skills and aptitudes possessed according to their unique vocation. I can have my own limits and frailty and sometimes make mistakes, but that doesn't take from me the right to be who I am and to exist according to my own personality. I am not someone extra in the world, and I do not feel guilty for existing. I can heal from this feeling that is so common today, the feeling of being an extraneous thing in the world, or feeling like existence is just pure chance.

Some say that this welcoming love of the child is first the province of mothers. Of course, a mother's role is very important. Nonetheless, I think we can dare to put it this way: it's more natural for a mother to welcome a child, whereas for a father it's less natural (maybe even difficult, sometimes), because for fathers it is more of a decision, a choice. The fact that it's a choice (and not merely by operation of nature) makes it all the more important that the words of a father welcome and validate the existence and proper identity of the child, recognizing it as his own son or daughter, which is something that gives the child an identity and certain rights under civil law.

The father—importantly though not exclusively—plays a role in mediating between the child and the world, in helping the child to find security and interior freedom and to advance through life with confidence. I think that this core of interior security, necessary for any person to feel free, is made up of a double certitude: the *certitude of being loved* and the *certitude of being able to love*. The loving presence of a father helps me acquire the certitude that I am loved with an unconditional love, a love that I cannot lose, a love on which I can always count, whatever may happen. But this doesn't suffice. To acquire the true interior security I need, I must also *know that I can love*. It's not sufficient to receive love; one must also give it. In spite of my limits and imperfections, I am sure of being able to love and of being capable of a disinterested love. I am capable of learning to love, of doing good around me, of giving my life lovingly for others. I can be a gift to others. This second certainty is as necessary as the first.

The presence of a father—his attitude, his care, his words (which don't have to be numerous)—can contribute immensely to engendering this double certitude in the child, whether a spiritual or natural one.

5

∽♥∿

A Father's Blessing

I would like to repeat these things in another way by mentioning a beautiful tradition that is present in Scripture and in human existence, which is the blessing of a father.

I often travel to Latin America. In many of these countries, when people know that you are a priest, they approach you and ask for a blessing: "*Padre! La bendición!*" Sometimes there is even a long line that forms!

This blessing request exposes a cultural reality, sometimes a little exaggerated but a just one nonetheless. It is valid, first, because it's not a man's blessing that the people are seeking but that of God, the Father of Heaven, and second, because this request manifests an attitude of humility on one hand (I am not self-sufficient, I need the blessing and grace of God in my life), on the other hand it shows simplicity and trust. Through the limited, poor figure of the priest (there is no sacrament here!), God can give his blessing, his love, and his well-being to his people. In Europe and North America this sort of request is rare, but this may be because we have grown prideful and have little faith.

In Judaism, after the Friday evening prayer of synagogue that heralds the Sabbath, on returning to the house, the father of the family blesses each one of his children. He also honors his wife in her role through the chanting of the *Eshet Hail*.[1] The importance of a father's blessing is quite prominent in the Old Testament.

This is also a tradition in many Christian families. When I was little, every night my father would come to the bed of each of his children to embrace them and bless them with a little cross on their forehead before they fell asleep.

This fatherly blessing is of great importance. The child who receives the blessing of his father feels loved as he is, has confidence in himself, and can confront life with courage and audacity, can take risks and make decisions. Life becomes a beautiful adventure. On the contrary, if he doesn't have his father's blessing, he will be less sure of himself, and life becomes difficult and complicated.

There's a passage from Scripture that is very meaningful to me in this regard. It's a text from the prophet Malachi that's found at a key point in Catholic Bibles,

---

1. Praise of the perfect woman in the book of Proverbs, 31:10–31.

because they are the last words of the Old Testament before the New Testament begins: "Behold, I will send you Elijah the prophet before the great and terrible day of the Lord comes. And he will turn the hearts of fathers to their children and the hearts of children to their fathers, lest I come and smite the land with a curse" (Mal 4:5–6).

What this text seems to signify in a very strong way is that, when the hearts of fathers are turned toward their children, and the hearts of children toward their fathers, then there is no curse. Human existence is beautiful and happy. On the other hand, when the hearts of fathers are not turned toward their children, or when the hearts of children are turned away from their fathers, there is a sort of curse on human existence; it becomes complicated and difficult.

We know that this passage from Malachi is taken up again in the Gospel of Luke when speaking of John the Baptist's mission (see Lk 1:16), because he is the prophet Elijah who was supposed to come. The role of John the Baptist is to prepare the way for Jesus and for the whole New Covenant, whose fundamental grace (through the mission of Jesus and the gift of the Holy Spirit) is to make us understand how completely God's heart is turned toward us, in love and mercy, and to invite all of us to turn our hearts toward the Father with the trust and love of children. Through Jesus, God becomes our father and we his children. Remember the words of the resurrected Christ to Mary Magdalene: "Go to my brethren and say to them, 'I am ascending to my Father and your Father, to my God and your God'" (Jn 20:17). Through the death and the resurrection of Christ, in a definitive, total way, God becomes our God and our Father.

I think that it's very meaningful that this message addressed to the apostles, summarizing the whole work of redemption and the mystery of God's fatherhood, is given to a woman. It's an indication of women's extremely important role in the salvation story by welcoming divine paternity and the restoration of human paternity.

Through the mission of the Son and the Spirit, in the mystery of the New Covenant, God reveals more deeply his fatherly love and gives everyone the power to become a child of God (see Jn 1:12).

In this vein, human fatherhood is made capable of being a symbol for God's fatherhood. Jesus, through his Spirit, comes to save, heal, and restore all types of paternity (and sonship). He takes up, purifies, rectifies, sanctifies human fatherhood, restoring its capacity to be a symbol of divine fatherhood. Human fatherhood, including that of the priest, is a *saved* fatherhood—saved by regaining its source and its model in divine fatherhood.

In a beautiful passage from his Letter to the Ephesians, Paul speaks about his mission to announce "the unsearchable riches of Christ, and to make all men see what is the plan of the mystery hidden for ages in God who created all things. . . . This was according to the eternal purpose which he has realized in Christ Jesus our Lord," a project that permits access to God in "boldness and confidence." It's interesting to note that in the same breath he also alludes to the mystery of earthly fatherhood: "For this reason I bow my knees before the Father, from whom every family in heaven and on earth is named" (Eph 3:8–15).

All human fatherhood finds its origins, its truth, and its finality in the fatherhood of God. The social and psychological work performed in this domain is necessary and praiseworthy, but insufficient. It's only in returning to God that human fatherhood can regain its true meaning and be exercised in a fair and fruitful manner.

6

What Makes for True Fatherhood?

Fatherhood, like all deep realities of human life and spiritual life, is obviously not something that we can imprison by words or definitions. All the more so if "every family"—and thus all fatherhood—"in heaven and on earth takes its name" from God, as St. Paul just told us.

There are, nonetheless, without pretending to unveil the mystery, some certainties that we can describe.[1] It seems to me that we can recognize fatherhood by two essential elements, which must not be unlinked from one another: unconditional love and the authority of the word.

Unconditional Love

Being a father means being a witness to the absolute and unconditional love of God for all people. This love,

---

1. A very interesting, deep reflection on fatherhood, from both an anthropological and a theological view, is Xavier Lacroix's *Passeurs de vie: essai sur la paternité* (Paris: Bayard, 2004).

which Paul speaks of in his first letter to the Corinthians, is one that "bears all things, believes all things, hopes all things, endures all things" (1 Cor 13:7).

All of us, whatever our errors or wounds may be, must feel welcomed and loved as we are. The father never has an attitude of rejection, disdain, hardness, or judgment against another. He even has special affection for the smallest, the poorest, the most hurting. He has a limitless patience, founded on hope. He believes the other, even when the other doesn't believe him. I would dare to say, supported by Paul's text above, that a kind of "unconditional hope" is one of the aspects of this unconditional love.

I heard a story about a man who was raised in a Christian family but rejected Christianity as an adult and refused to set foot in a church. Many years later he wound up returning to the faith and to practicing his religion. He said that he always believed that if he ever came back to the Lord one day, it would be because his father had never doubted him. His father always believed that one day his son would return to God.

It seems to me that here is a beautiful and deep dimension to fatherhood: never losing hope for those whom God confides to us as children, whatever may arise. I firmly believe in the strength of hope. "We get from God as much as we hope for," St. John of the Cross said. And

God tells us in Holy Scripture that those who hope in him will never be disappointed (see Is 49:23 and Rom 5:5).

Keeping a hopeful watch on others obviously isn't easy. But this hopeful gaze is a source of life. The father, through attitude, words, and the watch he has on those who belong to him, must not discourage but always be encouraging, helping them to believe in themselves and in their possibilities, in spite of their frailties or errors.[2] He must never give them a negative view of themselves, but instead demonstrate trust in them. This doesn't mean that the father is freed from helping others perceive what may be harmful or sinful in themselves. It's sometimes necessary to admonish, even to punish. Only the truth sets us free. But this must always be done with trust in God's mercy, which is greater than any evil, and in the hope that good can come of all.

To be a father means sometimes hoping against hope, as St. Paul says when he mentions the fatherhood of Abraham (see Rom 4:17–18). Which is to say: I may have a thousand reasons to lose hope in my child, but I hope nonetheless!

---

2. In human couples, the two partners must witness to this mutual care. Without listing a division of tasks, which would be absurd, perhaps what we can say is that maternal love is more charged with expressing unconditional love, while paternal love is more charged with keeping unconditional hope.

Fatherly love can be expressed in several ways: gestures, words, attitudes, but especially looks. The Gospels show us the importance of Jesus' gaze: "And Jesus looking upon him loved him" (Mk 10:21). God's beholding us is so beneficial, it frees us from the opinion that others have of us or that we have of ourselves, which is often a deprecating one. I think that the regard of a priest has a particular force, a certain authority, to give trust to others to have confidence in themselves.[3]

Words of Authority

The other essential dimension of fatherhood, inseparable from the first, is the capacity of transmitting a truth, of being the bearer of words of authority, of being a witness to something required, which is not about crushing, dominating, or controlling others, but is about helping others grow, becoming free and mature.

Thanks to his role, the father is clothed with a certain grace of authority, not at all in the sense of domination, but in the sense of service to enable others to grow. This theme is a delicate one because of all the abuses of authority that have become familiar. It's clear that we can't put fathers—or even priests for that

---

3. See the beautiful homily of Pope Francis on the Gospel of Matthew's vocation, which shows the force of Jesus' regard in making one free. Homily of September 21, 2015.

matter—on a pedestal as we sometimes did, which allowed some of these abuses to grow. But that doesn't mean that we should deny that a certain grace falls on fatherhood, a certain participation in the force of the Divine Word.

This is the domain of education, where the goal is to break free from sterile, egotistical attitudes and their infantile sources; from their limitations on perceiving reality; from the fears that can enclose us; and from the lack of trust and courage that prevents us from throwing ourselves into life and assuming our proper responsibilities.

The father encourages others to discern God's call in their lives and to respond to this call with trust and audacity, to fully become themselves, deploying all that is best in themselves. He communicates the words that give truth and force to free us from whatever may be holding us back from living fully.

We know that in the realm of family relationships, the presence of the father helps the child to avoid a relationship of dependency on the mother, helping the child to become autonomous and to hurl himself into life. The erasing of a father's role—I might even say of masculine virtues themselves, such as courage, combativity, strong-mindedness, uprightness—is not healthy. I'm not saying that women are not gutsy or courageous;

sometimes they are more so than men.[4] It's impossible to admire too much those women who raise their children alone. But I think that it's still the case that there's a kind of weakening of a man's role and of the masculine virtues in our world in favor of more feminine virtues (such as protection, tenderness, and compassion), and that this comes at the risk of introducing a type of "maternal" education, where we seek too avidly to avoid all pain, suffering, or combat, thereby giving way to a tendency to overprotect children. The end result is the formation of children who are insecure, fragile, and incapable of accepting suffering and frustration, which are traits indispensable for becoming an adult. This is not to mention the fact that eliminating the father weakens the role of the mother, too.

---

4. I am going to be accused of regurgitating gender stereotypes in speaking about masculine and feminine virtues. It is clear that men and women must practice both types. But it's still also true that each gender has a symbolic vocation to witness to certain dimensions of humanity. Only when taken together do masculine and feminine express all that is human. Just as Xavier Lacroix said, it's in relationship to each other that the masculine and the feminine are revealed, and this is done reciprocally. Affirming the fullness of equality between man and woman while at the same time giving all due regard to sexual difference—which is much more than just a cultural construction and which presupposes a certain differentiation in roles—is one of the world's current great challenges, and this challenge extends to the Church. It's one that must be addressed, without making the whole question merely one of power.

Our God is a merciful God, full of tenderness. His heart is more loving than the most tender of mothers. However, we all experience how this mercy does not procure for us a comfortable and easy existence, but instead makes us adults, capable of rising to the challenges and conflicts of life.

7

Failures in Fatherhood

Fatherhood is not an easy role to assume. It is, as we well know, subject to many failures, of various types, both in the human and the spiritual domains. Let's take a look at the principal ones.

Absence

The first failure is absence. Absence can sometimes create wounds that are as deep as those caused by paternal severity or abuse. It is the case of the father who doesn't take up his responsibilities. In the human realm, it means leaving the entire burden of children on the mother by refusing to assume his proper role. The absent father is one who doesn't dedicate time to his children, who isn't present or attentive as he should be, who never finds a moment to speak or play with them. He is always consumed by other tasks and is rarely at home.

The same applies to priests. I heard this reflection once, in a traditionally Catholic country: "Priests are always busy, occupied by a thousand activities. We can't ever speak with them, and when they give you ten minutes to listen, they're always looking at their watch!"

Of course, it wouldn't be just to generalize this complaint, but there is sometimes real suffering when the faithful are faced with a lack of availability, listening, or attention on the part of their pastors. This is not always an easy issue for priests to navigate themselves, because they are often overextended and there are people who are capable of devouring hours of their time, which they must protect against. That being said, our priests should ask for the grace of the Lord to know when to be attentive and available to those he entrusts to us. We are sometimes required to look at our watches to avoid arriving late to an important event, but looking at it while speaking with someone can be hurtful and can give the impression that our time is being wasted, that we have something more important to do than listen. Even if we can only give a little time to someone, we should convey the feeling—and it must be sincere—that, at that moment, the most important thing in the world is for us to be with that person.

The need for attention and listening is a very deep need for many. Fatherhood is first of all about presence. This presence doesn't need to be unrelenting (a child needs to breathe freely from time to time!), but it needs to be a quality presence in moments of encounter, and a presence that can be counted on in case of need. The father doesn't have to be there all the time, but when he is there, offering a sympathetic ear and a caring presence, the child knows that when the need arises, he can count on his father.

Severity

Another failure is the type of fatherhood that is too demanding and severe, crushing the child. Here, the father is never satisfied, asks for too much, and excites a feeling in children that they are never up to his expectations. Children are always reminded of their limits, insufficiency, and errors. They never receive congratulations or compliments. In the priestly realm, we can be guilty of expecting more of people than God asks of them!

It's good to remind ourselves from time to time of Jesus' words regarding the doctors of the law and the Pharisees in the Gospel of Matthew: "They bind heavy burdens, hard to bear, and lay them on men's shoulders; but they themselves will not move them with their finger" (Mt 23:4).

I remember a reflection I heard from a woman some years ago in another historically Catholic country. "During the whole period of my youth, almost every Sunday," she said, "I came back from Mass a little sad. The moralizing homily from the priest always gave me the impression that I wasn't a good-enough Catholic, that I wasn't up to the standard that God expected of me." The situation here is a delicate one: it's not about changing the gospel to make it agreeable to someone. Of course, we must preach it with all its force and its demands, but at the same time we must avoid making it a burden for the faithful to carry rather than the good news which it should never cease to be. Our words ought to encourage people and not discourage them. Encouragement is the proper foundation for the Holy Spirit.

Chumminess

Another deviation from paternity is the attitude of the priest who is content to be a friend, a buddy, without ever relating as a father. The priest who exhibits this weakness is really kind and close to everybody and knows how to make parishioners laugh during his homilies, but is in the end boxed into the "friend zone," failing to communicate to those in his charge anything that pushes them to grow and to convert. Among this group I would place some school chaplains I knew during the 1970s, who were very close to the students, dressing like them and going to the movies with them, without realizing that we, the students, expected something more from them: not just to be a buddy (we already had enough of these!) but to be a priest, someone who had something meaningful to tell us. A good friendship and a warm relationship between a shepherd and his sheep is an excellent thing, but it's not sufficient.

I must, however, recognize with gratitude that, during this very same peculiar period of the seventies, God led me to meet, among the chaplains at the University of Nancy where I was studying math, a Dominican priest named Chauvat, who was really a father for me and for many others. He is the one who helped me discover, among other gifts, St. Thérèse of Lisieux. He gave conferences on her writings at the chaplaincy, which was original for the time, when we were more likely to speak about politics, union engagement, sociology, or psychoanalysis than spirituality.

The Superman

Before moving on to more serious things, I don't want to forget in the list of disfigured fatherhood what I will call the "Superman father." This type is a person with many good qualities, a person who is apparently without reproach. He tries to make sure that no one ever perceives any vulnerability in him. I'm not saying that a father should lick his wounds and expose his faults; there are a lot of things that ought to remain personal and not be placed as burdens on children. But it's also necessary to be simple and truthful. A young man told me some time ago that the fact that he observed some weakness and vulnerability in his own father was in a certain sense reassuring. A perfect father—or rather one who doesn't want to let go of a perfect image—can in the end wind up distancing himself from his children. They need to feel that he is good, strong, assuming his responsibility for educating them with surety, but also vulnerable like any human being.

The Businessman

A frequent disfiguration of fatherhood is that of the priest who, more than being a father, is a businessman. Put another way, what counts for him are tasks to be completed: the construction of a new parish center, the embellishment of the church, or the deployment of a pastoral plan that he has concocted for his parish. These works are legitimate, necessary ones, but we run the danger of giving them priority. This leads to evaluating people according to their utility for such and such a task: to the effective, competent person who can help me complete this project, I will give a lot of attention, whereas one who is not talented and who has no utility for my plans may feel put aside. Instead of recognizing in each person, even the poorest among us, someone who deserves all my attention because the Lord loves them with a unique love, the businessman-priest judges him on exterior criteria involving competence and gain. Remember Jesus' words in the Gospel concerning children (which also apply to any person who is poor and fragile): "See that you do not despise one of these little ones; for I tell you that in heaven their angels always behold the face of my Father who is in heaven" (Mt 18:10). Each person has an absolutely unique connection with the mystery of God, which I must look beyond the limits of human sight to discern. As a priest, I am not called primarily to complete works, but to help each person to recognize and welcome the unique love that the Father has for them.

Power

Another deviation from true fatherhood is the search for power, the exercise of authority not as disinterested service but as domination. All forms of clericalism, authoritarianism, or abuse of power fall into this category, and unfortunately these can also be found in the Church. We've forgotten Jesus' words: "Whoever would be first among you must be your slave" (Mt 20:27); and those of Paul: "For though I am free from all men, I have made myself a slave to all" (1 Cor 9:19).

We all have a compelling need for recognition: the desire that our personality have force, value, and a certain glory. This is a legitimate need, but it often seeks its satisfaction through ambition, the desire to be first, a yearning to ascend the hierarchy, or the exercise of power over others. It makes authority, as conferred by God or by the Church, not just a humble and disinterested service but an expansion of *me*. We all are too well aware of the dramatic consequences. It leads us to keep people in a state of dependence instead of leading them toward freedom. We get attached to people rather than exerting ourselves to lead them to God. Instead of leading them into adulthood, we keep them in childhood. We make it so that they always need us, even when it would be better for them to be autonomous.

In his work *The Living Flame*, St. John of the Cross has some terrible words for spiritual directors who don't respect the particular and unique path of each soul, for those who exercise the tyranny of imposing their own conceptions of the spiritual life, keeping their protégés in a state of dependence and sometimes being more jealous of them than husbands are of their wives. "Thou art thus become a tyrant of souls, the robber of their liberties," he writes, "This is not zeal for the honor of God, but the zeal which cometh out of thine own pride and presumption."[1]

---

1. *The Living Flame of Love*, stanza 3, verse 64. *https://archive.org/stream/a588512100johnuoft/a588512100johnuoft_djvu.txt.*

A great example of pure and disinterested fatherhood is given to us by John the Baptist in chapter 3 of the Gospel of John. When the crowds little by little ceased to come and be baptized by him, preferring Jesus, and it troubled some of his disciples, John, on the contrary, rejoiced: "No one can receive anything except what is given from heaven. You yourselves bear me witness, that I said, I am not the Christ, but I have been sent before him. He who has the bride is the bridegroom; the friend of the bridegroom, who stands and hears him, rejoices greatly at the bridegroom's voice; therefore this joy of mine is now full. He must increase, but I must decrease" (Jn 3:27–30).

To be a father means not imposing myself on the other, but to the contrary allowing myself to decrease, to diminish, so that Christ grows in the other.

If we don't have this view, we wind up participating in one of the worst types of disfigurations of fatherhood. Instead of being disinterested, it becomes a way of using a person so as to fulfill our own human needs for recognition, ambition, or emotional, sentimental, or sexual satisfaction. It's pointless to expand on this, as there are countless painful current examples of people—priests, leaders, and founders of communities—for whom fatherhood was twisted into an abusive use of those placed in their trust. We remember the prophet Ezekiel's reproach addressed to the bad shepherds of the people of Israel, who exploited the people instead of taking care of them:

> Son of man, prophesy against the shepherds of Israel, prophesy, and say to them, even to the shepherds, Thus says the Lord God: Ho, shepherds of Israel who have been feeding yourselves! Should not shepherds feed the sheep? You eat the fat, you clothe yourselves with the wool, you slaughter the fatlings; but you do not feed the sheep. The weak you have not strengthened, the sick you have not healed, the crippled you have not bound up, the strayed you have not brought back, the lost you have not sought, and with force and harshness you have ruled them. So they were scattered, because there was no shepherd; and they became food for all the wild beasts. My sheep were scattered, they wandered over all the mountains and on every high hill; my sheep were scattered over all the face of the earth, with none to search or seek for them. (Ez 34:2–6)

There are no doubt other things to say on the possible deviations of fatherhood, but this suffices. To be a father, a lot of humility is required, a lot of disinterestedness and putting oneself second. It's a very demanding position. It's also a path of poverty. (We'll come back to this later.)

8

The Children's Problems

Before going further, I must remark that the ambiguities and possible difficulties in the father/son relationship don't only come from the father's side, but also from the children's side. Several types of problems are common.

A priest recounted to me that, in a parish where he was assigned as a young priest—a parish that was already deeply affected by the attitudes that sprang forth from the events of May of 1968 in France (a period of intense social and political unrest)—the first words that the lady in charge of the sacristy said to him were: "Don't count on me to call you 'Father'! I prefer to call you by your name." We aren't always surrounded by people who welcome the idea of fatherhood!

Among the forms that refusal of fatherhood takes, there is the "rebel child" in constant opposition with the father. We all know people with this kind of personality, who seem to need to oppose or protest something. It's the way that they've found to affirm themselves, a way that isn't always healthy.

There's also the type that is too dependent, that doesn't want to take the risk of freedom, of making a decision. In spiritual direction, we sometimes run across those who, because of their fears, their lack of trust in themselves, are more than happy to have someone else decide for them. They would rather unload the responsibility and risk of freedom on another, and so have a tendency to ask the spiritual father to make all decisions for them. We're obviously not doing them any favors by accepting this role.

We could also speak of the jealous child, who always feels as though he isn't the object of enough attention and love like his brothers and sisters are. This is the case of the elder brother in the Prodigal Son story, who believes, wrongly, that he is less loved than the younger brother because of the mercy that the younger one receives.

All of this is to say that, when we are a father, whether a human or spiritual one, we must expect to encounter attitudes that can be disconcerting, or not always easy to manage, from those entrusted to us by God. Every parish priest, for example, will have to deal with these types of attitudes from his flock from time to time: childlike dependence, rebellion without cause, jealousy. We must try to manage these problems as best we can, which isn't always easy.

9

Fatherhood in Scripture

Holy Scripture reveals the most beautiful and profound truths on the subject of fatherhood: divine fatherhood as well as human fatherhood, which are really so connected to each other, as Paul says in his letter to the Ephesians quoted above. I don't have the space in this short work (or the competency, for that matter) to develop this theme in a deep way. I've already alluded to certain Bible passages, so I'd just like to add a few references from texts or biblical figures that can help us understand what it means to be a father.

Fatherhood is a great mystery—even an unfathomable one—because it finds its origins in the very being of God. What is most profound about God is his merciful fatherhood. It exists in the eternal act in which the Father engenders the Son. It is manifested over the course of human history by the work of the Creator. God is the generous, abundant source of life, creator of everything—God who, according to Paul's words, "gives life to the dead and calls into existence the things that do not exist" (Rom 4:17). It shows itself in his redemptive work, as we saw above in quoting Isaiah.

Human fatherhood is also far from being merely biological, psychological, or social. It is also a spiritual mystery. The Bible offers some particularly meaningful figures here who are worthy of our attention.

Abraham

Abraham is a wonderful figure of human and spiritual fatherhood. He reminds us right away that paternity is not founded on possession so much as dispossession. Abraham couldn't become a father except through a miracle of divine mercy, given his age and the sterility of Sarah. What's more, we could say that Abraham became fully father of his son Isaac only after he consented to offer him in sacrifice and Isaac was given back to Abraham by God. These facts remind us that paternity in its most definitive sense is not a personal capacity or a human power that we can claim but is rather a pure gift of grace.

What's more, this fatherhood of Abraham—fatherhood of his son Isaac through the flesh (but also fatherhood of a much larger group through all believers)—is essentially a mystery of faith, as St. Paul's passage in the letter to the Romans says: "As it is written, 'I have made you the father of many nations'—in the presence of the God in whom he believed. . . . In hope he believed against hope, that he should become the father of many nations; as he had been told, 'So shall your descendants be'" (Rom 4:17–18).

It is not in a human capacity, but really much deeper in an act of faith and hope that all authentic fatherhood finds its expression and its fruitfulness.

This is the experience that parents have sooner or later. Fatherhood, as well as motherhood, even if their beginning point is a biological or psychological reality, must always at some point become something spiritual, living out the role on a deeper level than a merely human one. This comes especially during moments of trial, when, in spite of their role as father or mother, parents can no longer help a child who has asserted their own independence and no longer listens to them, following paths that are not those that the parents may have wanted. At this point, fatherhood and motherhood are at a moment of poverty, powerless to help the one they love with all their being, which is a hard trial to go through. But it's also a chance to become still more deeply involved in the role: crying out to God, praying without ceasing, persevering with trust. The only resources that remain available at that point to regain the child and continue nonetheless in the role of father or mother (in a poorer way, sorrowful but still fruitful) are those of faith, hope, love, and prayer.

Moses

Moses is another wonderful figure from the Old Testament who exhibits spiritual fatherhood, in the role he was given from God to free the people from slavery in Egypt and to lead them to the Promised Land, through a long and difficult path of learning. This fatherhood was a heavy load, and Moses himself often complained of it to the Lord, as in the passage where the people were grumbling because they only had manna to eat and they wanted meat:

> Moses heard the people weeping throughout their families, every man at the door of his tent; and the anger of the Lord blazed hotly, and Moses was displeased. Moses said to the Lord, "Why hast thou dealt ill with thy servant? And why have I not found favor in thy sight, that thou dost lay the burden of all this people upon me? [12]Did I conceive all this people? Did I bring them forth, that thou shouldst say to me, 'Carry them in your bosom, as a nurse carries the sucking child,' to the land which thou didst swear to give their fathers? Where am I to get meat to give to all this people? For they weep before me and say, 'Give us meat to eat.' I am not able to carry all this people alone, the burden is too heavy for me. If thou wilt deal thus with me, kill me at

once, if I find favor in thy sight, that I may not see my wretchedness." (Num 11:10–15)

Other than the fact that it was sometimes hard to bear, like any father of a household or any priest, I would make two other remarks on the subject of Moses' fatherhood.

The first is that another passage from the Book of Numbers says this beautiful thing about Moses: "Now the man Moses was very meek, more than all men that were on the face of the earth" (Num 12:3). The Hebrew adjective used here, *anav*, means both sweetness and humility. It's interesting that the Scripture tells us that this great leader in salvation history was the most sweet and humble person on the earth. This is an essential characteristic of fatherhood, and we'll come back to this.

My second remark is that Moses' fatherhood is exercised in several ways—leading the people, nourishing them, protecting them, educating them—but especially through intercessory prayer. When the people fight against Amalek on the plain, Moses prays on the mountain, his arms elevated toward God, thus obtaining the victory (see Ex 17:8–16). When the people commit a sin of idolatry by creating the golden calf and God wants to destroy them, Moses obtains their forgiveness from God through his intercession (see Ex 32:1–14). He goes so far as to say to God in his prayer: "Alas, this people have sinned a great sin; they have made for themselves gods of gold. But now, if thou wilt forgive their sin—and if not, blot me, I pray thee, out of thy book which thou hast written" (Ex 32:31–32). Moses asks God to erase him from the Book of Life rather than to refuse pardon to the people. Can you conceive of a more pure and self-less love?

In a beautiful homily on the intercession of Moses and the role of the pastor as an intercessor who makes himself a "bridge" between God and his people, Pope Francis said, "Thus, the manner of prayer most proper to Moses is through *intercession*. His faith in God is completely at one with the sense of fatherhood he feels toward his people."[1] Here we notice again this link between faith and fatherhood that we mentioned with Abraham.

Saint Paul

In the New Testament, the apostle Paul seems to be a beautiful example of priestly fatherhood. He claims this fatherhood with regard to the community at Corinth:

> I do not write this to make you ashamed, but to admonish you as my beloved children. For though you have countless guides in Christ, you do not have many fathers. For I became your father in Christ Jesus

---

1. General Audience of June 17, 2020.

through the gospel. I urge you, then, be imitators of me. Therefore I sent to you Timothy, my beloved and faithful child in the Lord, to remind you of my ways in Christ, as I teach them everywhere in every church. (1 Cor 4:14–17)

Paul was aware of having engendered the life of Christ in those to whom he proclaimed the gospel. He didn't hesitate to call Timothy "my beloved child," as he also did with Titus, "my true child in the faith" (1 Tim 1:2).

The most beautiful text from Paul's letters on this theme is the passage from the First Letter to the Thessalonians, where he expresses his love for the community he is addressing. Here we find note of true fatherhood: force, affection, gentleness, tenderness, solicitude, generosity, purity, and absolute selflessness. And, like any true spiritual fatherhood, Paul's love also has some maternal accents:[2]

For we never used either words of flattery, as you know, or a cloak for greed, as God is witness; nor did we seek glory from men, whether from you or from others, though we might have made demands

---

2. St. Francis of Sales didn't hesitate to use the expression "a paternally maternal affection." Letter to St. Jane Frances de Chantal, 1331.

as apostles of Christ. But we were gentle among you, like a nurse taking care of her children. So, being affectionately desirous of you, we were ready to share with you not only the gospel of God but also our own selves, because you had become very dear to us.

For you remember our labor and toil, brethren; we worked night and day, that we might not burden any of you, while we preached to you the gospel of God. You are witnesses, and God also, how holy and righteous and blameless was our behavior to you believers; for you know how, like a father with his children, we exhorted each one of you and encouraged you and charged you to lead a life worthy of God, who calls you into his own kingdom and glory. (1 Thess 2:5–12)

In a similar way, Paul expresses his paternal love with the most sorrowful expressions for the churches in Galatia that were in the process of distancing themselves from the gospel as preached by the apostle, returning to circumcision and to the prescriptions of Jewish law, risking loss of the Christian freedom Paul had given them access to: "My little children, with whom I am again in travail until Christ is formed in you! I could wish to be present with you now and to change my tone, for I am perplexed about you" (Gal 4:19–20).

We notice a strong emotional dimension in Paul's spiritual fatherhood. It is good for the priest (who is so much more than just a civil servant!), and also for his flock, who needs this loving warmth. We must not, amidst all of today's problems, lose this dimension. The emotional disorders that exist today invite us to exercise prudence and purity of love, but should not cause us to be fearful of loving. I remember meeting an auxiliary bishop from a big American diocese who tried to keep his position as a parish priest as well, in order to maintain a concrete link with the faithful. I was touched to notice that, when he celebrated Sunday Mass, I could perceive his deep joy at being among his people, like a father surrounded by his children, and also the affection of the faithful for their pastor.

We must not let prudence and respect become coldness. People need affection and to love and be loved.

There are many other people or texts from the Bible that we could meditate on regarding the subject of fatherhood. I have already mentioned the parable of the Prodigal Son. There is also everything that Jesus said about his relationship with the Father (particularly in John's Gospel), as well as his attitude toward people. Jesus is the Son, but he also exhibits a certain paternity, in a discreet but real way, toward his disciples. He never ceases instructing and educating them; he defends them when they are criticized by the Pharisees. In the apparition by the lake related by John, the resurrected Christ addresses the disciples by calling them "children" (Jn 21:5).

A wonderful figure of fatherhood that we must not forget is St. Joseph. His was a fatherhood that was not founded on sexual procreation but was nonetheless a very important spiritual and human fatherhood. He is the earthly father that the Savior himself needed. Joseph was a righteous man, prone to silence and prayer, with a total devotion to those the Lord entrusted to him, especially Mary and Jesus; a man of obedience and faith, perfectly chaste in his affection, capable of unforeseen and courageous decisions when the Lord asked them of him. He is certainly a saint to be imitated and invoked, as much by fathers of households as by priests, to help them exercise their fatherhood.

I will stop my biblical meanderings here, even if they were very limited and incomplete on the subject.

PART TWO

—⟨∾⟩—

A Profound Transformation of Heart

10

~~~

How to Become a Father

The question to ask ourselves after the preceding reflections is the following: How does one become a true father, a father according to the gospel, a person who is an authentic image of divine paternity? What is the spiritual path that allows our human heart to become the heart of a father, in the image of God's heart?

It's not just about applying a practical recipe, putting some methodology in place. It's about a profound transformation of heart that only the Holy Spirit is capable of effecting. We will also consider a number of points from our concrete lives that favor this interior transformation, the progressive configuration of our hearts into the sweet and humble heart of Jesus.

To Be a Father, You Must Be a Son

The first affirmation, an absolutely essential one that I'd like to elaborate on here, is this: we cannot truly be a father without first being a son.

We must be a son above all in our relationship with God. The spiritual fatherhood that we are trying to develop is not just a human work, one that we can achieve purely by our own efforts. It is more like a grace, something to ask for and to receive, a participation in the ineffable paternity of God. This presupposes entering into an ever more intimate sonship with God. Jesus is the example of the son who gives himself totally to the Father and who is fully open to the gift of the Father's grace. With the clear awareness that I am nothing on my own, I situate myself as totally dependent on and welcoming of God.

We must be like Jesus in his relationship with the Father, receiving everything from him: his identity as a son, his mission, and the necessary grace to accomplish this mission. We must enter into this filial trust and abandonment, this total receptivity to God—receiving one's self and receiving everything from the Father. It's a way of being that should leave its mark on all aspects of our existence, but that is expressed in a special way in prayer, and is deepened continually.

The Gospels (Luke in particular) speak to us often about Jesus' prayerful devotion, which had really impacted his disciples. These were long periods of prayer, away from the crowds, in the desert or out-of-the-way places, to which Jesus submitted himself. He was entirely given to his mission during the day, but very early in the morning, or after having sent the crowds away in the evening, the Lord spent long hours praying to the Father. The disciples called him out on this, coming to ask Jesus: "Lord, teach us to pray, as John taught his disciples" (Lk 11:1). That's when he taught them the Our Father, which is so much more than a formula; it's a whole manner of being.

The disciples didn't know what Jesus was living through or saying in his prayers, but they felt strongly how important this time of prayer was, and how it was principally through prayer that the Savior, in offering himself to the Father, received everything from him: his life, his identity, his mission, grace and light and wisdom, the strength to go on, the power to heal, the supernatural authority that he possessed.

We cannot become a father without this faithfulness to prayer, these prolonged sessions that keep us in the presence of God, offering ourselves to him and receiving from him, like little, poor, dependent children, knowing with certainty that we will obtain from the very hands of our heavenly Father everything that we need. We must also be conscious that only prayer will give authority to our teaching.

It is also at the feet of the Blessed Sacrament, in daily faithfulness to moments of Eucharistic Adoration, that the priest truly becomes a father. This is where the Father of heaven communicates his true fatherhood, his compassion and his tenderness for all his children. This is where, in large part, one acquires the attention for others that one needs. One of the fruits of prayer is a greater share of this quality of presence for others. In being attentive to God in adoration, we also learn to be attentive to others. Being present for God in adoration helps us be present for others. We learn to make people our priority, not letting ourselves be seized by the activism that makes us businessmen rather than fathers. The priest can heal from all the deformations of fatherhood and rectify little by little the attitudes that aren't right, the "worldliness" of which Pope Francis speaks. Here we learn to love with a pure and selfless love (we can't persevere in faithful prayer and simultaneously be obsessed with ourselves). Here, pastoral charity is cultivated in our hearts.

The closer we are to God, the more we can be close to men, with a closeness that's both loving and respectful. The priesthood is blessed with this double gift of proximity with God and proximity with all of us, the two reinforcing each other. The closer I am to God, the more I can make myself truly a neighbor of each person. Conversely, it's also clear that the more attentive I am to those that God entrusted to me, the closer I am to the Lord himself.

We can never overemphasize the importance for a priest of living in prayerful intimacy with God; from this proceeds the fruitfulness of the priestly state. A priest who doesn't pray will never be a true priest. During the first years of ministry, there might not be an obvious difference between a priest who is truly faithful to his times with the Lord and one who doesn't pray or prays insufficiently. But after ten or twenty years, the difference is stark. The Christian people can easily tell when a priest is a man of prayer and when he isn't. They trust the first type a whole lot more than the second.

I am fortunate to be part of a community (the Community of the Beatitudes) whose rule of life requires me to spend an hour each day in silent Eucharistic Adoration. I believe that the Lord couldn't give me a greater gift. My prayer is often poor, but this is where I find peace, strength, and the light I need for my ministry.

On Holy Thursday 1979, in the first letter that he wrote to priests after his election as sovereign pontiff, Pope Saint John Paul II highlighted the essential importance of a life of personal prayer for priests, particularly as a way of permanent conversation:

Being converted means to pray continually and to never lose heart (see Lk 18:1). *In a certain way, prayer is the first and the last condition for conversion*, spiritual progress and holiness. Perhaps in these recent years—at least in certain quarters—there has been too much discussion about the priesthood, the priest's "identity," the value of his presence in the modern world, etc., and on the other hand there has been too little praying. There has not been enough enthusiasm for actuating the priesthood itself through prayer, in order to make its authentic evangelical dynamism effective, in order to confirm the priestly identity. *It is prayer that shows the essential style of the priest; without prayer this style becomes deformed.* Prayer helps us always to find the light that has led us since the beginning of our priestly vocation, and which never ceases to lead us, even though it seems at times to disappear in the darkness. Prayer enables us to be converted continually, to remain in a state of continuous reaching out to God, which is essential if we wish to lead others to him. Prayer helps us to believe, to hope and to love, even when our human weakness hinders us.[1]

---

1. Pope John Paul II, Letter of His Holiness John Paul II to All of the Priests on the Occasion of Holy Thursday 1979 (April 18); second emphasis added. Vatican website: *www.vatican.va*.

Being a Son and Groom of the Church

The priest, to be a father, must also be a "son of the Church." The priesthood conferred on him, and the paternity that he's clothed in little by little, are not his personal property but are given to him by the Church.

This presupposes a love of the Church, being in deep communion with her and her leaders. It also means recognizing with gratitude how much I owe to the Church. In spite of her imperfections and the sin that can mark some of her members, it's through the Church that I've received everything: my baptism, my identity as a child of God, my priesthood. It's in the Church and by her mediation that I've received divine life and that I can introduce other people into the divine life.

In the natural domain, just as a woman can't become a mother without the grace of a spouse, a man cannot become a father without the grace of a spouse. In an analogous way, a priest can only become a father through the mediation of the Church, and through being a spouse to her, in loving her with this spousal love—a love that Paul speaks of when he describes marriage and evokes the love of Christ for the Church. "Husbands, love your wives, just as Christ loved the church and gave himself up for her, that he might sanctify her, having cleansed her by the washing of water with the word" (Eph 5:25–26).

This love of the Church and this communion with her doesn't dispense us from the need to be lucid about sin and the need for reform, and to contribute to that reform. We do so not from an exterior, critical view, but as a member attached through sonship to what is, in spite of its failings, the Bride of Christ. Today there's a lot of talk about "repairing the Church," but we must not forget that we can only renew the Church at the price of deep conversion and personal purification, and with unfailing solidarity with the Church. A priest who is always criticizing the Church and its representatives, or who is quick to speak poorly of his bishop, will never become a true father.

The history of the Church shows us that the people who most contributed to the renewal of the Church and to its purification (St. Francis of Assisi, St. Catherine of Siena, and many others) never had the pretention of being reformers, and were always motivated by an immense love and great respect for the Church. They challenged the way that members of the Church lived, sometimes forcefully,[2] but not its fundamental structure.

---

2. Catherine reproached some cardinals for being "mute dogs," silent instead of warning when the pack was in danger. But at the moment of her death she said: "the only cause of my death is the love of the Church which burns in me and consumes me." Let's also not forget her beautiful words: "Take your sweat, take your tears, and collect them at the source of my divine charity, and with them in union with my other servants, wash

While Christianity was divided between a pope and an antipope, Catherine of Siena had the audacity to call the legitimate pope "sweet Christ on the Earth."

I recently read a review for a book that proposed nothing short of eliminating ordination as a solution for problems with the priesthood. I don't think that this is the right path. It is better to help a sick person regain health than to make him disappear.

Our Mother Church allows the priest to become a father in conferring on him the sacramental grace of the priesthood, giving him the ability to administer the sacraments, sending him out to preach the gospel, and making him a pastor and guide for the Christian community. It's in exercising these three responsibilities that are proper to the priestly state—the three duties of teaching, sanctifying, and governing—that the priest can deploy his spiritual paternity.[3]

Here there's a remark to be made: we must recognize that, in the daily practice of priestly ministry,

---

the face of my Bride. I promise you that this remedy will reveal her beauty. It is not the sword, nor war or violence that will reveal her beauty, but peace, humble and stalwart prayer, sweat and tears shed with ardent desire by my servants" (Letter 367 to the Queen of Hungary). [Translator's note: Translation mine]

3. See the teaching of Pope Benedict XVI during the general audiences of April 14, May 5, and May 26, 2010, on these subjects (the tasks of teaching, sanctification, and government in priestly ministry).

it's the Christian people entrusted to our care who, through the needs that they bring to us and the requests they make, really make us become fathers, little by little. We know that in all families it is, in the end, the children who educate the parents, making them fully become fathers and mothers. It's the same for us priests. Without a concrete community of believers entrusted to us, believers who ask things of us all the time, obliging us to give more than we had expected to give and to go beyond what we are inclined to do on our own, we would never be capable of becoming true fathers. We can't be fathers on our own; we can become them only in relation to the faithful. It is they who engender in us spiritual paternity. It's the church community that makes fathers out of us! There is a wonderful reciprocity between the priest and his people: by our fatherhood we introduce believers into divine life, but they are the ones who, by their needs and requests, their support and their prayer, induce priestly fatherhood in us.

On the human as well as the spiritual level, no one is fruitful on his own; there is no possible fruitfulness except in the mystery of union—union with God, union between people, union with the Church. This is one of the great illusions of our modern culture's individualism: believing that human persons can fulfill themselves on their own. It can only be done in the context of union, communion, and faithfulness with others.

Let's conclude in remembering that priestly fatherhood, if it finds its roots and primary expression in the ecclesiastic community, shouldn't be limited to this. Like the heavenly Father's love, it should embrace the entire world: believers and nonbelievers, those who are close and those who are far off.

Being a Brother

To be a son of God also means recognizing and welcoming all people as brothers and sisters. We can't be a father if we are not first a brother: in charity, simplicity, humility, and a spirit of service.

I am a brother, first, with all my fellow priests. The priesthood that I've received, the fatherhood that is derived from it, is not my private property but is a gift that I've received and that I share with all other priests, whether it be in the context of a diocese, in the religious community that I'm a part of, or in whatever other ecclesial context I exercise my ministry. The capacity to maintain friendly, respectful, reciprocally collaborative relationships, and of looking up to other priests, is fundamental for developing an authentic spiritual paternity. A priest with a tendency to criticize his brothers frequently, or who pits them against himself in rivalry or competition, cannot become a father and will never be accepted as one by others.

It seems to me that one of the most destructive things for priestly fatherhood is to compare oneself in a spirit of judgment or rivalry with regard to other priests. It might be a prideful tendency to imagine that I have the better parish, the most beautiful church, the most magnificent liturgy, or the greatest number of youth frequenting Mass. This is unfortunately a common mindset. For example, how many cases of "bell tower quarrels" are there in Church history, of jealousy and competition among ecclesial groups or religious communities? On the contrary, we should practice what St. Paul said to the Romans: to "outdo one another in showing honor" (Rom 12:10).

In the urgent situation of today's world, it's really necessary to know how to collaborate with other people or ecclesial entities, freeing ourselves from any spirit of comparison or competition, like members of one body. A lot of communities or movements have lost out because of the illusion of being better than the others. Some communities that claimed to be saving the Church were in the end saved by it!

I would like to remind you of something about Teresa of Avila. We know that she never said anything bad about anyone. As a result, everyone trusted her and opened their hearts to her easily. It's clear that if a priest has a tendency to criticize others, people will have difficulty opening up to him. They're going to think: if he speaks poorly of others, one day he'll also speak poorly of me! Don't forget that the person who criticizes or condemns always winds up discrediting himself. It's inescapable.

If I am a priest, it's also fitting to be a brother to all people, the laity in particular, with whom I am called to collaborate. Without renouncing, of course, the specific gift that was made to me, which is the fatherhood that I am called to assume, I must avoid any form of clericalism, any attitude of superiority owing to my knowledge, my function, or any other capacity that may be mine. Being above all a pastor, I am first and foremost a simple brother in Christ. I must avoid absolutely any haughtiness or disdain, like the Pharisees or Sadducees from the Gospel who disdained those who were less educated.

Living in the Spirit of the Beatitudes

Becoming a father presupposes a path of conversion, a deep transformation of heart, a passage from a worldly mentality to the truth of the Gospel, evoked for example by St. Paul in the Letter to the Romans: "Do not be conformed to this world, but be transformed by the renewal of your mind, that you may prove what is the will of God, what is good and acceptable and perfect" (Rom 12:2).

It seems to me that the best description of the interior itinerary that we should be keeping in order to exercise authentic paternity is found in the text of the Beatitudes from St. Matthew's Gospel.

Jesus' words in this passage are addressed to all believers, of course, whatever their vocation may be. But it seems that they can be interpreted as a way to foster the blossoming of priestly spiritual paternity.[4]

> *Blessed are the poor in spirit, for theirs is the kingdom of heaven.*
>
> *Blessed are those who mourn, for they shall be comforted.*
>
> *Blessed are the meek, for they shall inherit the earth.*
>
> *Blessed are those who hunger and thirst for righteousness, for they shall be satisfied.*
>
> *Blessed are the merciful, for they shall obtain mercy.*
>
> *Blessed are the pure in heart, for they shall see God.*
>
> *Blessed are the peacemakers, for they shall be called sons of God.*
>
> *Blessed are those who are persecuted for righteousness' sake, for theirs is the kingdom of heaven.*

---

4. For a more detailed commentary on the Beatitudes, see my book *The Eight Doors of the Kingdom: A Meditation on the Beatitudes* (New York: Scepter, 2018).

Blessed are you when men revile you and persecute you and utter all kinds of evil against you falsely on my account. Rejoice and be glad, for your reward is great in heaven, for so men persecuted the prophets who were before you. (Mt 5:3–12)

Let us now comment on each beatitude to show how each of them enlightens the conditions that make true fatherhood possible. We'll spend the most time on the first one, which is the foundation of all the others.

11

Living the First Beatitude

❖ BLESSED ARE THE POOR IN SPIRIT FOR THEIRS IS THE
  KINGDOM OF HEAVEN.

In all types of fatherhood, there exists the essential mystery of poverty. It is impossible to be a father without a true poverty of spirit, which means accepting a radical dispossession of self, a profound interior emptying.

This is something that appears clearly when we consider the parable of the Prodigal Son and the merciful father in chapter 15 of Luke's Gospel. In this story, everyone claims something: the young son claims his part of the inheritance; the older son claims justice because he believes that he was treated unfairly by the father. The only one who claims nothing for himself is the father. He is poor in spirit. He is the one who goes out to the others: he runs to welcome the young son at his return when he sees him from afar; he leaves the house to go speak to the older son when he is angry and refuses to come in to take part in the feast. He asks for nothing for himself. The only thing he desires is the good of his sons: that the lost son be saved, and that the older one abandon his anger to rejoice at the return of the younger one. He imposes nothing on them, he only proposes. He considers his material things to be of little value—as he does his honor, his dignity, even his own suffering. The only important thing in his eyes is the good of his children.

The mystery of poverty is a constituent part of all fatherhood, human or spiritual. This is what makes it so difficult! A man is not always excited to assume his role as father. It's easier to cling to the claims of the childlike or adolescent position. There's a cost in renouncing any form of advantage to one's self, one's own requirements and possessions.

Poverty of spirit as it relates to fatherhood has various aspects. We will look at some of them.

Looking Out for the Other Before Self

When we become fathers, when children are entrusted to us, we become poor. We can no longer live for ourselves but must live for another. It is no longer our own interests that are the most important things, but those of the child. We are no longer autonomous; we become a dependent of those who depend on us. The man who becomes a father must submit to this new, fragile life that has been put in his hands. It is this little one who becomes the master! It is often the little ones, with their needs, who decide the daily program of life. It's the same with spiritual fatherhood. "The poor are our masters," Vincent de Paul used to say.

In general, it is somewhat natural for a woman to be a mother. Being a father is more difficult, because it involves a decision: not being content merely with having made a child with a woman (a thing that doesn't take a whole lot of effort!) but recognizing this child as my son or daughter, taking up my responsibility as a father. This requires a decision, words of recognition, an engagement of my will. The little child asks me a question that I am called to answer: What will you do with me? Are you going to take care of my needs, welcome me and love me, provide my food, give me a roof to live under, protect me?

And there's another, still more radical question: What education will you give me? What values will you transmit to me?

This means that human fatherhood always directs us to something bigger than ourselves. It points to something transcendent. What fundamental and universal human truths am I going to communicate to the child? Toward what vital meanings will I orient his or her growth? What God will I propose that they adore? Worldly idols or the true and living God?

Assuming a fatherly responsibility, I become poor in my time and in my personal projects. I must consent to this with love. This poverty is a grace, for it invites me to enter into the mystery of love. It impels me to practice Jesus' words from the Gospel: "For whoever would save his life will lose it; and whoever loses his life for my sake, he will save it" (Lk 9:24). But it's sometimes painful to consent to this. Children are a great gift, as they make me come out of myself and my natural egocentricity. "Lord, make us understand that we won't arrive at fullness of life except through constant death to ourselves and our egotistical desires," Mother Teresa of Calcutta said.

It is in educating others that we grow ourselves, in taking care of others that we realize ourselves and achieve the depth and beauty latent in our own lives.

In the spiritual domain, it's in transmitting the spiritual values to others—the truth of the gospel—that these values take on all their beauty, light, and force. There's something paradoxical in the ending of Mark's Gospel: the resurrected Jesus scolds the disciples for their lack of faith and stubbornness, and just after this he tells them to "go into all the world and preach the gospel to the whole creation" (Mk 16:15). He knows full well that it is precisely by proclaiming the gospel to the world that their own faith will be strengthened.

Dispossessing the Self and Welcoming the Other

As we said about Abraham, fatherhood is not a possession but to the contrary, a dispossession. Others are entrusted to me for a time, but they don't belong to me in any case. I have a responsibility for them, and I exercise legitimate authority for this purpose, but it must be exercised with respect for who they are, their own identity, unique vocation, and stage of growth. These are realities that are always unique and different from what I might project or imagine. Today's current expression, "parental project," is extremely ambiguous. Being a parent implies renouncing any preconceived project for children so as to let them become themselves. The human person can never be enclosed into a project, whatever it may be. A human person is too vast. This respect requires a renouncement, a refusal to impose on others our ideas, our desires, or our plans. Children are never what we would like them to be. It is hard to accept, but it is a gift: it will lead to an enlargement of our thoughts, our heart, our wisdom. Leaving our schemes behind opens us to the diversity and surprising richness of life. Life is always richer than we think or expect.

Consenting to Our Limits and Exhausting the Resources of Faith

There is another kind of poverty in fatherhood, which is derived from the fact that the relationship that I establish with the other in the concrete exercise of fatherhood, like any deep relationship (for example, the husband/wife relationship), inevitably leads to the revelation of my own poverty. Loving others, putting myself at the service of their needs, respecting them in the vocation and identity that is proper to them, and educating them, are not after all such simple things. They require an internal labor, by which I realize my poverty and limits. Loving others just as they are, helping them in an effective way, helping them grow spiritually and humanly, are not as easy as might be imagined. Every young couple beginning the education of their children thinks that they will do better than their own parents did. We think it is sufficient to apply ourselves to the task with some good principles and it will work! After a few years, we are often obliged to realize that we have not done better than our parents![1]

Daily activity with the person I am responsible for reveals my limits, maybe even a part of the sinfulness

---

1. See the prophet Elijah's reflection during a time of "depression:" "It is enough; now, O Lord, take away my life, for I am no better than my ancestors" (1 Kings 19:4).

that is within me: lack of gentleness, patience, mercy, and so forth. How easily do I get discouraged, annoyed, or angry? As a father, whether spiritual or human, we always find a son or a daughter who will drive us to our limits, who knows the art of unhinging us, of pushing us into our darkest corners. Being a father confronted by your children is sometimes a very humiliating experience.

On a deeper level, I would add that once we are led to exercise spiritual fatherhood or motherhood, introducing people into a life of grace, we always end up perceiving that it's an impossible task. It's impossible to do good to others, to give them exactly what they need; it's a project that is too difficult for us. St. Thérèse of Lisieux, when she had to begin to take care of some of the younger sisters that had been entrusted to her by the mother prioress, put it this way:

> From a distance it appears all roses to do good to souls, making them love God more and molding them according to one's personal views and ideas. At close range it is totally the contrary, the roses disappear; one feels that to do good is as impossible without God's help as to make the sun shine at night. One feels it is absolutely necessary to forget one's likings, one's personal conceptions, and to guide souls

along the road which Jesus has traced out for them without trying to make them walk one's own way.[2]

What must be done when faced with this experience? Accept our own radical poverty, and put all our trust in God alone. Continue to do what we can humbly and faithfully, leaning on the Lord with a great spirit of faith. If we are of good will, if we learn to set aside our personal views, the Holy Spirit will come to the aid of our weakness, and the grace of God will do its work.

What It Means to Be Poor

I would like to develop a point here that, to me, seems essential, for priests in particular: the deep link between poverty of spirit and the spirit of faith.

What does it mean to be poor? It means not being able to rely in the end on anything but God; having no other security than our faith and our hope in the Lord; the impossibility of relying on ourselves, our capacities, our conceptions, our wisdom, our formation, and counting on God alone. The holy Curé of Ars said,

---

2. Thérèse of Lisieux, *Manuscript C*, folio 22v. Page 265 in the *Oeuvres Complètes* Cerf DDB. This chapter (folios 22 to 25) where Thérèse describes the way she played her role as the mistress of novices (without having this title) is an enlightening example of a strong, disinterested, pastoral love. [Translator's note: Quotation from: *http://archives-carmel-lisieux.fr/english/carmel/index.php/c21-30/c22/c22v*]

"God gave me the great mercy of not putting anything in me that I can rely on: no talent, no knowledge, no wisdom, no strength, no virtue."[3]

This doesn't mean that the realities that I just mentioned (capacities, formation, competencies, acquired wisdom) are useless or disdainful things. Not at all; it is right to acquire them. We must make use of them but not create a safety net of them. We must use them but always in a way that, in the end, we rely on God alone and on his mercy, which really supports us.[4] It's not always easy or natural to do (we really want to lean on our own riches!), but in the end it's a source of freedom and peace. Thérèse of Lisieux puts it this way: "We experience such great peace when we're totally poor, when we depend upon no one except God."[5]

---

3. Jean-Marie Vianney, *Pensées* presented by Bernard Nodet, Artège, p. 260.

4. As St. John Eudes invites us: "Do not rely on the power or influence of friends, on your own money, on your intellect, knowledge or strength, on your good desires and resolutions, or on human means, or on any created thing, but on God's mercy alone. You may, of course, use all these things and take advantage of every aid that you can marshal on your side to conquer vice, to practice virtue, to direct and conclude all the business that God has placed in your hands, and acquit yourself of the obligations of your state in life. But you must renounce all dependence or confidence you may have in these things, to rely upon Our Lord's goodness alone." (*The Life and the Kingdom of Jesus*) [Translator's note: Quotation from: *http://www.liberius.net/livres/The_life_and_kingdom_of_Jesus_000000343.pdf*]

5. Yellow notebook, August 6, 4. [Translator's note: Quotation from: *http://archives-carmel-lisieux.fr/english/carmel/index.php/carnet-jaune/2320-carnet-jaune-aout*]

We should make use of our human capacities, but the ultimate support is our faith, our absolute trust in the faithfulness and mercy of God. This is what a spirit of faith consists of: seeing the hand of God in everything and relying absolutely on him.

We find a beautiful illustration of this "spirit of faith" in the life of Paul, particularly in the fourth chapter of the Second Letter to the Corinthians.

After having spoken about the beauty of the ministry he received from God's mercy—the New Covenant, a ministry even more glorious than Moses'—Paul reminds us that his ministry was entrusted to fragile beings, that this treasure is carried in earthen jugs, pottery without value, human people who are continually in a situation of distress and precariousness:

> But we have this treasure in earthen vessels, to show that the transcendent power belongs to God and not to us. We are afflicted in every way, but not crushed; perplexed, but not driven to despair; persecuted, but not forsaken; struck down, but not destroyed; always carrying in the body the death of Jesus, so that the life of Jesus may also be manifested in our bodies. For while we live we are always being given up to death for Jesus' sake, so that the life of Jesus may be manifested in our mortal flesh. So death is at work in us, but life in you. (2 Cor 4:7–12)

This surprising description of the apostolic ministry that Paul gives is, I believe, the most exact one we can find. The apostle is not an indefatigable superman who is sure of himself and who easily dominates all situations, but a man constantly at the limit of his capacities, who stays the course only out of pure grace. He is, according to his own words, being "put to death" all the time, but staying the course all the same!

What is it then that makes him persevere? It is the spirit of faith, as he goes on to explain:

> Since we have the same *spirit of faith* as he had who wrote, "I believed, and so I spoke," we too believe, and so we speak, knowing that he who raised the Lord Jesus will raise us also with Jesus and bring us with you into his presence. For it is all for your sake, so that as grace extends to more and more people it may increase thanksgiving, to the glory of God.
>
> So we do not lose heart. Though our outer nature is wasting away, our inner nature is being renewed every day. For this slight momentary affliction is preparing us for an eternal weight of glory beyond all comparison, because we look not to the things that are seen but to the things that are unseen; for the things that are seen are transient, but the things that are unseen are eternal. (2 Cor 4:13–18, emphasis added)

The apostle could have come up with a thousand good reasons to be quiet, to renounce his ministry: his interior frailties, his imperfections, or the many exterior difficulties he encountered. In spite of all of that, *he speaks*, animated by the spirit of faith! He gives himself to his ministry, sustained by his faith, which makes him see the invisible, and by his hope in the Resurrection.

If someone were to ask me what I think is the most important quality in a priest, I would say, of course, being faithful to the teaching of the Church, that it is pastoral charity.[6] But I would add right away that this pastoral charity, in order to endure and to multiply, desperately needs a foundation, something to give it strength, which is nothing other than the spirit of faith. Without faith, love gets discouraged and dries up pretty fast.

Whatever may be our personal weaknesses and imperfections, whatever may be the external difficulties that we may encounter in our ministry, the priest must always remain a man of faith. He must never doubt his call, the value of his ministry, the fruitfulness (even if it remains invisible) of his vocation. The biggest risk that a priest runs is to doubt his priesthood.

---

6. See the apostolic exhortation by John Paul II, *Pastores dabo vobis* (March 25, 1992).

I have gone through difficult times in the Church during the years that followed the Second Vatican Council. I was a seminarian in Lyon in a religious congregation that I entered when I was eighteen years old. The Church in France went through a profound crisis, which, in my opinion, was above all a crisis of priests. Many left the ministry at this point. The priest who was my spiritual director when I was studying philosophy in 1968 left the congregation at the end of the year to get married. Not very encouraging for the youth that we were.

We can't judge anyone, of course, and that's not what I intend to do here. But I think that the problem in the end was that a lot of priests had begun to doubt their priesthood. They no longer perceived any sense to it. They had the impression of being behind in a sort of societal evolution, and they didn't see that, as priests, they had a lot to give this world that was in the midst of big changes. Why did this happen? For varied and complex reasons: the lack of a solid spiritual life; the lack of good philosophical and theological formation, necessary to face new problems that required delicate discernment; and strong pressure from the surrounding society, among others. I think that this was also a time of fierce spiritual warfare.

The priest must obviously be a man who is filled with humility, without any arrogance or feeling of superiority in regard to anyone else. But he must also be, like

Paul, convinced of the beauty of the ministry that God's mercy has entrusted to him, without ever doubting, in spite of his weakness, the grace that falls on him, and he must lean on this grace with trust. Of course, this trust must not become presumption, something that leads him to neglect working seriously on his own conversion. The priest must live his mission in as holy a way as possible, in a state of constant conversion, but always in a spirit of great trust. "He who calls you is faithful," St. Paul says to the Thessalonians (1 Thess 5:24).

There's another aspect of this spirit of faith that I don't want to forget: believing that everything is in God's hands. All the circumstances we go through, whatever their cause may be, good or bad, are in God's hands, and everything can work toward good if we love him, according to Paul's words (see Rom 8:28). In the end, the spirit of faith is really the principal quality of Christ's ministry. It is a faith full of humility and gentleness and is a constant path of conversion, but it doesn't allow itself to be torn down by anything, by any failure or difficulty.[7]

---

7. See the words of the Council document on the life and ministry of priests: "The divine task that they [priests] are called by the Holy Spirit to fulfill surpasses all human wisdom and human ability. 'God chooses the weak things of the world to confound the strong' (1 Cor 1:27). Aware of his own weakness, the true minister of Christ works in humility trying to do what is pleasing to God. Filled with the Holy Spirit, he is guided by him who desires the salvation of all (*Presbyterorum Ordinis*, no. 15).

Our worst sin is not our human weaknesses or miseries (God knows very well how to make use of them!) but our lack of faith in the fidelity and power of God.

Spiritual Poverty and Humility

An essential aspect of spiritual poverty is humility: recognizing that we are nothing and that we can do nothing on our own, but that everything is freely given out of God's mercy.

"The Almighty has done great things in the soul of the child of his divine Mother, and the greatest was having showed it its littleness, its weakness," Thérèse of Lisieux said.[8]

We must consent to a complete dependence on God's grace. This is the way we can receive grace most abundantly. There is nothing like humility for attracting the grace of the Holy Spirit. "God opposes the proud, but gives grace to the humble," St. Peter said (1 Pt 5:5).

We shouldn't attribute to ourselves the good that we accomplish, or use it to inflate our ego, claiming a victory for us. Instead we should attribute it, with thanksgiving, to God, who is the only source of good.

Another aspect of poverty of heart means not thinking that the good that I do, or my generosity in

---

8. Manuscript C.

service, gives me particular rights with God or others. This is the point of the parable of the useless servant in Luke's Gospel.

> Will any one of you, who has a servant plowing or keeping sheep, say to him when he has come in from the field, "Come at once and sit down at table"? Will he not rather say to him, "Prepare supper for me, and gird yourself and serve me, till I eat and drink; and afterward you shall eat and drink"? Does he thank the servant because he did what was commanded? So you also, when you have done all that is commanded you, say, "We are unworthy servants; we have only done what was our duty." (Lk 17:7–10)

This parable, which in our eyes may seem harsh, is really very freeing. It invites us to remain in our place as humble servants. It stops us from taking ourselves too seriously and shouldering what belongs to the Master. A Carmelite father once told me: "My priestly life changed the day I understood that I am not the savior!"

Jesus' words here also invite us to relinquish our claim on the good that we've accomplished. We have a tendency to think that the good that we've done for others confers on us some kind of rights over them, but this can completely falsify our relationship with them. We are no longer then within the logic of gratuity, of love.

The good that we accomplish is already a grace, a gift of God's mercy. We should not expect a reward for it. If we don't understand this, we'll always be unhappy and unsatisfied. We'll always be making calculations and comparisons, and we'll always be finding that we've done more than others and that we haven't received as much as we deserve. Have no fear. God will repay us infinitely more than we can imagine, but we have to stop worrying about claiming whatever it may be. Let our calculations, our claims and requirements of others, stop, and let us abandon them to God's mercy. It will be a lot more generous than our human generosity.

Humility is also about being reconciled with our own weakness. Let's revisit the words from the Curé of Ars: "God gave me the great mercy of not putting anything in me that I can rely on: no talent, no knowledge, no wisdom, no strength, no virtue."[9] We shouldn't see weakness as a handicap but as a great grace, since it makes us more dependent on God's mercy. It forbids pride and self-sufficiency from developing, and it forbids us from thinking that we're better than others and judging them.

This is what St. Paul had to practice regarding his famous "thorn in the flesh" (see 2 Cor 12:7), which

---

9. Jean-Marie Vianney, *Pensées* presented by Bernard Nodet, Artège, p. 260.

we don't really know much about. It's better this way because it allows each of us to recognize our own weakness, whatever it may be.

This humiliating human weakness, from which Paul suffered greatly, to the point that he asked three times for the Lord to deliver him from it (not out of a desire for well-being but because he feared that it was an obstacle to the fruitfulness of his ministry of preaching the gospel), was something Jesus asked him to accept: "My grace is sufficient for you, for my power is made perfect in weakness" (2 Cor 12:9).

I am convinced that there's a link between the beautiful spiritual fatherhood that we find with Paul and this experience of poorness that is consented to.

I'd like to make one final remark on this theme of poverty of spirit. The more a person has poverty of spirit, being gentle and humble, the more his words take on a true authority, a capacity to convince. It's paradoxical, but experience shows that it's true. What gives authority to our words is not being louder than others, or having more subtle or intelligent arguments, nor does it rely on our number of diplomas or the vast culture we exhibit. What does give it authority is when, in those words, there is no self-seeking, when they are totally disinterested, when they are never in service of our own interests but are only in the service of the truth.

12

Living the Rest of the Beatitudes

Having spoken of poverty of spirit at great length, let's move on to the remaining beatitudes.

❖ BLESSED ARE THOSE WHO MOURN, FOR THEY SHALL BE COMFORTED

The father is someone who knows how to make his children's suffering his own. Pope Francis, in his letter to priests on the occasion of the feast of the Curé of Ars, gave thanks for all the priests who "embody a spiritual fatherhood capable of weeping with those who weep."[1] We know St. Paul's words: "Rejoice with those who rejoice, weep with those who weep" (Rom 12:15). In the Second Letter to the Corinthians, when he witnesses to his constant worry for all the churches, he says this:

---

1. Pope Francis, Letter of His Holiness Pope Francis to Priests on the 160th Anniversary of the Death of the Holy Curé of Ars, St. John Vianney (August 4, 2019). Vatican website: *www.vatican.va.*

"Who is weak, and I am not weak? Who is made to fall, and I am not indignant?" (11:29).

This beatitude of tears calls us to open ourselves to God's consolation—not just to share the suffering of others as I mention above, but also to accept courageously our own cross, the inevitable weight of suffering that hangs on our shoulders for many reasons: the heaviness of tasks to accomplish, the fatigue, the battles of all sorts, difficulties and misunderstandings and the often-painful experience of our own limits.

Few among us can give a list of suffering as long and varied as Paul witnesses to in his letters, especially in chapter 11 of the Second Letter to the Corinthians, but each of us has our share. Paul doesn't bring up his suffering as an apostle to complain or ask for the pity of his listeners. To the contrary, he says: "Now I rejoice in my sufferings for your sake, and in my flesh I complete what is lacking in Christ's afflictions for the sake of his body, that is, the church" (Col 1:24). He speaks this way to give us courage. "Take your share of suffering like a good soldier of Christ Jesus," he says to Timothy (2 Tim 2:3).

If the cross is constantly present in Paul's life, he is also not missing God's consolation. In the first chapter from the Second Letter to the Corinthians, he gives thanks for this: "Blessed be the God and Father of our Lord Jesus Christ, the Father of mercies and God of all comfort, who comforts us in all our affliction, so that we may be able to console those who are in any affliction, with the comfort with which we ourselves are comforted by God. For as we share abundantly in Christ's sufferings, so through Christ we share abundantly in comfort too" (2 Cor 1:3–5).

In this typical Jewish-style prayer of thanksgiving, Paul uses one of the most beautiful designations that we can find for God—"Father of mercies and the God of all consolation"—and he witnesses to a remarkable experience: knowing how to submit to the many trials he encounters on his way, he finishes by experiencing the sweet consolation of the Holy Spirit, and he realizes that this consolation received from God is not for him alone but gushes forth to others, especially those in his care. Accepting his own cross, Paul receives divine consolation, and thus becomes a consoler for those who suffer. The suffering and weakness that he experiences at certain times gives him understanding of others; the help and consolation that he receives afterward from the Father makes him able to comfort others and give them words of hope. The sharper the suffering that is accepted and entrusted to God, the more powerful the grace that the apostle later benefits from to console his brethren.

It seems to me that this truth is a beautiful dimension of paternity. The father is a person who is spiritually an adult, who knows how to accept suffering and recognizes it not as a disaster but a grace. A father is not an infantile person, an "enem[y] of the cross of Christ" (Phil 3:18), as St. Paul called those who constantly dream of a more peaceful life (which really makes life tougher: a cross we refuse is much heavier than a cross we accept), but instead he is a person who accepts life in all its facets, its complexity, its occasional hardness, and who in the end receives the peace and comfort of God that he can then communicate with others.

There's a paradox here that at its deepest is a beautiful truth: accepting the cross makes us able to console others. The cross makes us poor, humble, gentle, compassionate, and merciful. It makes us similar to Jesus, who, because he was tried in all things, became able to share our weakness, as the Letter to the Hebrews says (see Heb 4:15).

It seems very important to me that the priestly ministry, especially today, be cloaked in the anointing of consolation. Being a consoler, a bearer of hope and peace, is part of the mission. The Gospel that is read during the Chrism Mass during Holy Week, when the priests unite around their bishop and renew their priestly engagement, is the preaching of Jesus in the synagogue in Nazareth at the beginning of his public ministry, where he reads the passage from Isaiah: "The Spirit of the Lord is upon me, because he has anointed me to bring good news to the poor. He has sent me to proclaim release to the captives and recovering of sight to the blind, to set at liberty those who are oppressed, to proclaim the acceptable year of the Lord" (Lk 4:18–19).

I am convinced that the faithful of today have much more need of consolation and comfort than reproaches. Reproach is sometimes necessary, but it should be given advisedly (don't require of others more than God asks of them) and in gentleness and peace.

Experience shows that the greatest danger to souls is discouragement. Our mission is a mission of encouragement.

❖ BLESSED ARE THE MEEK, FOR THEY SHALL INHERIT
THE EARTH

Humility and meekness are essential qualities for a priest to truly be a priest. If the priesthood involves the grace of configuring oneself like Christ, we should never forget that the essential qualities of Jesus' heart are meekness and humility, as he himself affirms in the wonderful passage from St. Matthew: "Come to me, all who labor and are heavy laden, and I will give you rest. Take my yoke upon you, and learn from me; for I am gentle and lowly in heart, and you will find rest for your souls" (Mt 11:28–29).

Gentleness and humility (as the opposite of hardness and pride) go together. In the Old Testament the same Hebrew word, *Anav*, means both humility and gentleness, which are the fruits of poorness of spirit. As we already said, this term is applied to Moses in the Book of Numbers: "Moses was very meek [gentle], more than all men that were on the face of the earth" (Num 12:3). Because Moses was poor in spirit, humble and meek, God could put so much into his hands; Moses was "entrusted with all my house" (Num 12:7).

As was the case for Jesus, the heart of the humble and meek person becomes a real place of repose for others: everyone feels profoundly welcomed and loved, everyone can abandon themselves to it and open up to it with trust and without fear. Everyone can be freely themselves without need to make efforts to feel accepted or understood. If the crowds pressed forward to Jesus, it is surely because of the healings that he accomplished, but also because of his meekness and humility. This is in contrast to the hardness and arrogance of the Sadducees and some of the doctors of the law, who disdained the ordinary people, criticizing Jesus for being a friend of tax collectors and sinners (see Mt 11:19).

Nothing is more precious for a priest than meekness and humility. There is a power in meekness. Pope Francis' words remind us of this as he speaks about Our Lady of Guadalupe to the bishops of Mexico at the Metropolitan Cathedral of Mexico City: "Above all, *la Virgen Morenita* teaches us that the only power capable of conquering the hearts of men and women is the tenderness of God. That which delights and attracts, that which humbles and overcomes, that which opens and unleashes, is not the power of instruments or the force of law, but rather the omnipotent weakness of divine love, which is the irresistible force of its gentleness and the irrevocable pledge of its mercy."[2]

In the exercise of his ministry, the priest must be attentive to avoiding any kind of hardness, inflexibility, or arrogance, and to showing himself to be truly a man of meekness and humility in the image of Christ and so many of the holy pastors that the Church has been blessed with over the ages. He cannot be a man who is prone to anger. This feeling is inevitable, or sometimes even legitimate, but we must remember what St. Paul said: "Do not let the sun go down on your anger, and give no opportunity to the devil" (Eph 4:26–27). We have the right to be angry sometimes, but never for more than a day!

This gospel-like meekness is opposed to hardness, to anger, to violence, but it is also opposed to bitterness. To keep bitterness in one's heart, to keep resentment by

---

2. Pope Francis, Address of His Holiness Pope Francis, Metropolitan Cathedral of the Assumption, Mexico City (February 13, 2016). Vatican website: *www.vatican.va*.

nurturing wounds is often a sign of hidden pride, and also of a lack of trust in God. These things end up hardening the heart and making it less accepting of others. Knowing how to forgive, accepting wholeheartedly every situation, accepting our weakness and poorness—these are the necessary attitudes for acquiring this interior meekness that is so precious in pastoral relationships.

❖ Blessed Are Those Who Hunger and Thirst for Righteousness, They Shall Be Satisfied

We find here one of the fundamental qualities of any true ministry of the gospel. The desire for righteousness is not just a moral or social reality. It's a spiritual reality first: the desire for holiness, the desire to conform fully to God's will, the desire for truth, the desire for permanent conversion. St. Anthony of the Desert, who died at the age of 106, said a few years before his death: "I have not yet begun to convert myself"!

Exercising fatherhood means having this hunger and thirst: we're never finished purifying ourselves, growing in love and mercy, dying to our egocentric self. The very exercise of fatherhood, like any deep relationship to another, is a constant provocation to a more radical conversion. We have a daily experience of this. We must consent to the difficult interior work that frees us little by little from all of our narrow-mindedness and small-heartedness.

I mentioned above how an essential expression of this thirst for conversion is faithfulness to prayer. Only God can give us this new heart that we need to be true fathers. We should cry out to him, bombarding him day and night with prayer and supplication.

A hunger and thirst for righteousness is also, of course, understood in its biblical sense—the ardent desire that all men and women be justified, that is to say, saved. A father ardently desires fullness of life for all his children. We should be constantly aspiring to commune with Jesus' thirst for the salvation of souls: "I came to cast fire upon the earth, and would that it were already kindled! I have a baptism to be baptized with; and how I am constrained until it is accomplished!" (Lk 12:49–50).

Like so many saints, we should ask that Jesus' cry on the cross, "I thirst!," deeply inhabit our hearts. Among several examples I could give, I would like to mention the spiritual experience that Thérèse of Lisieux lived through at the age of fourteen, of which she wrote in *Story of a Soul*:

> One Sunday, looking at a picture of Our Lord on the Cross, I was struck by the blood flowing from one of the divine hands. I felt a great pang of sorrow when thinking this blood was falling to the ground without anyone's hastening to gather it up. I was resolved to remain in spirit at the foot of the Cross and to receive the divine dew. I understood I was then to

pour it out upon souls. The cry of Jesus on the Cross sounded continually in my heart: "I thirst!" These words ignited within me an unknown and very living fire. I wanted to give my Beloved to drink and I felt myself consumed with a thirst for souls. As yet, it was not the souls of priests that attracted me, but those of great sinners; I burned with the desire to snatch them from the eternal flames."[3]

May the little Carmelite who prayed so much for priests during her life, and who continues to do so from the heavens, inspire in us the same ardent desire for the salvation of all people. This communion with Jesus' thirst is where all spiritual paternity or maternity finds its deepest thirst.

❖ Blessed Are the Merciful, for They Shall Obtain Mercy

We've already meditated on the link between fatherhood and mercy, notably with regard to the Prodigal Son and his merciful father. The priest is essentially a minister of divine mercy and of the infinite love of our heavenly Father, who tenderly attends to every human misery, corporal or spiritual.

---

3. Autobiography Manuscript A 45 back page. [Translator's note: Quotation from: *http://archives-carmel-lisieux.fr/english/carmel/index.php/41-50/45/45-verso*]

For this reason, the priest must be the first to know God's mercy and to experience it himself, taking up Paul's words in the First Letter to Timothy:

> I thank him who has given me strength for this, Christ Jesus our Lord, because he judged me faithful by appointing me to his service, though I formerly blasphemed and persecuted and insulted him; but I received mercy because I had acted ignorantly in unbelief, and the grace of our Lord overflowed for me with the faith and love that are in Christ Jesus. The saying is sure and worthy of full acceptance, that Christ Jesus came into the world to save sinners. And I am the foremost of sinners; but I received mercy for this reason, that in me, as the foremost, Jesus Christ might display his perfect patience for an example to those who were to believe in him for eternal life. (1 Tm 1: 12–16)

Being aware of his duty to divine mercy, by virtue of his vocation especially, a priest should rely on this merciful love with full confidence, burning with the cause of becoming the witness and minister of this love toward those entrusted to him. Through his teaching, the way he confers the sacrament of reconciliation, and his relationships with people, he should try to inspire everyone to have a greater trust in God's mercy, which is infinitely bigger than our sins.

Remember Jesus' words to St. Faustina: "Tell my priests that hardened sinners will repent on hearing their words when they speak about My unfathomable mercy, about the compassion I have for them in My Heart. To priests who proclaim and extol My mercy, I will give wondrous power; I will anoint their words and touch the hearts of those to whom they will speak."[4]

We are all called to be merciful to others, as God is with us—our God who "makes his sun rise on the evil and on the good, and sends rain on the just and on the unjust (Mt 5:45). This attitude is even more necessary for priests. If a priest doesn't have a merciful heart, he lives in contradiction with his vocation. He must be, like Jesus, "the face of the Father's mercy," according to Pope Francis' words in the encyclical announcing the Jubilee year of mercy *Misericordiae Vultus*.

In this beautiful text, the pope tells us that "Mercy is the very foundation of the Church's life. All of her pastoral activity should be caught up in the tenderness she makes present to believers; nothing in her preaching and in her witness to the world can be lacking in mercy. The Church's very credibility is seen in how she shows merciful and compassionate love." And he invokes John Paul

---

4. St. Faustina Kowalska, *Diary*, no. 1521. [Translator's note: Quotation from: *https://archive.org/details/St.FaustinaKowalskaDiary_201509/page/n335/mode/2up*]

II's words: "The Church lives an authentic life when she professes and proclaims mercy—the most stupendous attribute of the Creator and of the Redeemer—and when she brings people close to the sources of the Savior's mercy, of which she is the trustee and dispenser." He adds later: "Consequently, wherever the Church is present, the mercy of the Father must be evident. In our parishes, communities, associations and movements, in a word, wherever there are Christians, everyone should find an oasis of mercy."[5]

❖ BLESSED ARE THE PURE OF HEART, FOR THEY SHALL SEE GOD

We have already insisted on this point: there is no authentic fatherhood without a pure and selfless love, love that is not self-seeking but is at the service of the good of the other.

Having a pure heart means loving with this love that respects the other, that doesn't seek to dominate, possess, control, or use the other, as we have noted.

A pure heart, according to Scripture, is above all a heart that is not shared: shared between God and idols, shared between the spirit of the world and the spirit of

---

5. Pope Francis, *Misericordiae Vultus*—Bull of Indiction of the Extraordinary Jubilee of Mercy (April 11, 2015), nos. 1, 10–12. Vatican website: *www.vatican.va*.

the gospel. A pure heart is a simple heart, unified in the love and desire for God.

An essential aspect of purity of heart in relation to others is selflessness: loving others for themselves, not for any gain we may get out of it. "Let no one seek his own good, but the good of his neighbor," as St. Paul says (1 Cor 10:24).

This requires great respect: respecting others in their unique identity and their particular vocation, respecting freedom, emotions, intimacy, and body. It means avoiding any kind of manipulation, intrusion into the other's life, prying curiosity. It involves acknowledging that God's path for the other may or may not be the same as mine.

Approach others with delicateness, attention, respect—no matter what defects or problems they may have—like a holy land, which we can only approach by taking off our sandals, as Moses did when he approached the burning bush. Recognize in every person, even the most disfigured one, the divine presence, the face of Christ we are invited to love. Recognize that everyone is wanted by God, created out of love, and that Christ shed his blood for everyone. I already quoted Jesus' words: "See that you do not despise one of these little ones; for I tell you that in heaven their angels always behold the face of my Father who is in heaven" (Mt 18:10).

Fatherhood requires both a closeness and a distance: closeness in presence, tenderness, and concern for the other; but distance in respect and in non-invasion of the intimate space of another. This distance sometimes requires accepting a kind of solitude; I should not require the other to take care of my needs or respond to my wishes. I must acquire the maturity that allows me to find in God the things I need to satisfy my most fundamental needs: peace, security, fullness, and happiness.

This interior purity requires a long process of conversion and healing. It can only be the fruit of divine creation. "Create in me a clean heart," David says in his prayer of repentance (Ps 51:10).

The fruit of this purity is seeing God: seeing the face of God in the other, seeing the action of God in his life and also recognizing it in mine. We sometimes complain that God is too hidden, that he doesn't show himself in our lives. But maybe it's that our hearts aren't pure enough to recognize the discreet, humble, but real signs of his presence. We are often blinded by self-love, by our desire for reality to conform to our wishes.

One last remark to conclude on this point: one of the best ways to purify the heart is gratitude. Praise and thanksgiving purify the human heart because they turn it away from itself and turn toward God by expressing faith, hope, and love. Trying, in spite of difficulties, to live in constant thanksgiving will contribute greatly to keeping a pure heart, by not letting it be invaded by bitterness, discouragement, sadness, or anger. St. Paul frequently exhorts us to "be thankful" (Col 3:15): "Always and for everything [give] thanks in the name of our Lord Jesus Christ to God the Father" (Eph 5:20).

❖ BLESSED ARE THE PEACEMAKERS, FOR THEY SHALL BE CALLED SONS OF GOD

The peacemaker beatitude is the seventh. The figure seven in the Bible indicates fullness, an achievement. This reminds us that we can't find true peace except in living the six previous beatitudes. The Beatitudes are a path toward interior peace, the only true path that works.

If we are poor in spirit, humble and meek, capable of accepting suffering and of receiving divine consolation; if our most deep desire is to conform ourselves to the will of the Father; if we are merciful; if our love is pure and selfless; then we will find peace of heart, the peace that Jesus promised to his disciples: "Peace I leave with you; my peace I give to you; not as the world gives do I give to you. Let not your hearts be troubled, neither let them be afraid" (Jn 14:27).

It's very important for the priest to be a man of peace. The ministry entrusted to him is a ministry of reconciliation and peace, according to Paul's words:

All this is from God, who through Christ reconciled us to himself and gave us the ministry of reconciliation; that is, God was in Christ reconciling the world to himself, not counting their trespasses against them, and entrusting to us the message of reconciliation. So we are ambassadors for Christ, God making his appeal through us. We beseech you on behalf of Christ, be reconciled to God. (2 Cor 5:18–20)

Paul again evokes this mystery of reconciliation and peace in the letter to the Colossians: "For in him all the fullness of God was pleased to dwell, and through him to reconcile to himself all things, whether on earth or in heaven, making peace by the blood of his cross" (Col 1:19–20).

Thanks to the ministry of the Church, we are reconciled with God, reconciled with our neighbor, and thus find peace.

If he wants to exercise this ministry toward others, the priest himself must have received this grace of reconciliation and peace: he must be at peace with God (living in the freedom and joy of knowing that he is a child of God), he must be reconciled with himself (freely accepting his own weakness), and he must be reconciled with others (capable of accepting them as they are, forgiving their errors, holding no grudges against anyone).

He must also be reconciled with life: accepting life as it is, not being bitter or resentful toward existence. Even if life's paths are sometimes dark, painful, or deceiving, he must always maintain this trust that the Lord, like a good shepherd, "leads me in paths of righteousness for his name's sake" (Ps 23:3).

It seems to me that the deepest meaning of the seventh beatitude could be expressed like this: blessed are those who are capable of welcoming and keeping in themselves the peace of God, in order to transmit it later to others— not spreading fear, worry, division, agitation, or bitterness around themselves, but radiating the great, kind, divine peace. May all our lives be a conduit of the Risen Christ's gift to his disciples: "Peace be with you" (Jn 20:19).

The priest cannot be a man of conflict, of incessant debate with others. He has the right, of course, to speak his mind in the controversies that may agitate the world or the Church, but he should never have a partisan or hostile attitude, being "against" whatever it may be. We can be opposed to ideas, and that is sometimes necessary, but we must not be opposed to people. A real father cannot be against any of his children, even if they're wrong.

Being a peacemaker also supposes self-mastery with language. We can't be a father and simultaneously someone who gossips too much. A father knows when to speak but also when to keep silence. He is capable of holding his tongue, first of all out of respect for those who confide in him and who count on his discretion, but also to avoid leaning on others with his own battles or worries. We should speak with people who can accompany us and help us, but not with just anyone. Fathers must be vigilant about this need that we sometimes have for sharing our difficulties or for justifying ourselves. We are in a world that speaks too much, that has the illusion that the more we speak of problems the better they are resolved. There are of course questions that require debate to find good answers. But often, speaking too much about difficulties makes them harder to bear. Difficult situations also require silence, interior rumination, and prayer to be confronted in the right way. We must know when to take the time to regain peace before expressing ourselves, in order to avoid doing something in the heat of emotion. Remember Paul's words: "Let no evil talk come out of your mouths, but only such as is good for edifying, as fits the occasion, that it may impart grace to those who hear" (Eph 4:29).

The peace of the seventh beatitude is also the biblical *shalom*, the peace of the seventh day, the Sabbath day, the day when God rested after the work of creation. This peace is given to us when we know how to repose in God. In the existence of every Christian, especially a priest, there is the paradox of a life filled with combat, struggle, and suffering to announce the gospel, but at the same time a profound peace, the peace that is not a human creation but the fruit of communion with Christ and the result of putting ourselves in the Father's hands. It is a peace that comes from abandoning ourselves to him, from trust, prayer, and the moments when we respond to St. Peter's invitation to "cast all your anxieties on him, for he cares about you" (1 Pt 5:7), to be like a child who sleeps in the arms of his father. I like Thérèse of Lisieux's expression from one of her poems: "I want to love you like a little child, I want to fight like a valiant warrior."[6]

This repose, this sabbath of the soul, that God can use to be present with us, is celebrated in Psalm 62: "For God alone my soul waits in silence" (verse 1); and in Psalm 16: "my body also dwells secure. For thou dost not give me up to Sheol, or let thy godly one see the Pit" (verse 9–10). The Letter to the Hebrews reminds us that it is especially our hardness of heart, our lack of faith and trust that prevents us from entering into God's repose (see Heb 3–4). Here we encounter again the importance of faith that I have already spoken of.

Even during difficulties and tempests, we must conserve the peace of God as much as possible in our hearts

---

6. Poem 36. [Translator's note: Translation mine]

in order to transmit it to others. This requires being deeply rooted in faith and prayer. We often regain the peace we lost through adoration of the Blessed Sacrament. It is when we put ourselves entirely in the hands of the Lord and when we make contact in faith with the presence of God, who is an ocean of peace, that heavenly peace descends into our agitated hearts.

This is what allows us to confront suffering or agitation in others without letting it destabilize ourselves. It's not always easy. It often happens that in our ministry we must be face-to-face with people going through strong emotions: anger, fear, bitterness, despair, or sadness—things that aren't always easy to overcome. The Prodigal Son's father had to confront his older son's anger. We must be capable of not just having the grace of human experience (even though learning to listen in a human way is indispensable) but also of having the grace of deeply rooted faith and hope. We must witness to great empathy, a great capacity to accept the suffering of others, letting ourselves be touched by their suffering ourselves, but without letting it trouble us and without losing our objectivity by taking part in it in a way that isn't right. For that, it's necessary to conserve our peace, an interior stability, founded on faith—a faith that can lead us into even the worst situations with a hopeful outlook.

❖ Blessed Are Those Persecuted for Righteousness' Sake

"Blessed are those who are persecuted for righteousness' sake, for theirs is the kingdom of heaven. Blessed are you when men revile you and persecute you and utter all kinds of evil against you falsely on my account. Rejoice and be glad, for your reward is great in heaven, for so men persecuted the prophets who were before you" (Mt 5:10).

What link can we establish between this beatitude of those persecuted for the kingdom and the mystery of a priest's spiritual fatherhood?

We've already underlined the difficult fatherly task that requires struggle, suffering, and spiritual combat in particular for learning to love with a pure love. Some sorrows are certainly not childlike. What's more, in this great struggle for life, the Adversary will often be there to tempt, discourage, accuse, and torment those who, in spite of human limitations, sincerely try to exercise the fatherhood entrusted to them as well as possible. He who wants to be a father according to the gospel will not always be understood and will sometimes suffer for the truth.

It seems to me that one aspect of this beatitude is an invitation to accept injustice sometimes, consenting to our lot, which means not always being loved, respected, or considered as we may wish to be. We know St. Peter's words from his epistle:

For one is approved if, mindful of God, he endures pain while suffering unjustly. For what credit is it, if when you do wrong and are beaten for it you take it patiently? But if when you do right and suffer for it you take it patiently, you have God's approval. For to this you have been called, because Christ also suffered for you, leaving you an example, that you should follow in his steps. He committed no sin; no guile was found on his lips. When he was reviled, he did not revile in return; when he suffered, he did not threaten; but he trusted to him who judges justly. (1 Pet 2:19–23)

Peter tells us bluntly that part of the Christian vocation means sometimes submitting to injustice. We must not be surprised, but consent to it and find the necessary strength for this by contemplating Jesus' example.

It seems to me that there's a certain applicability here to the domain of fatherhood. There is, we could say, in the exercise of fatherhood a certain baseline injustice that we must consent to. The love of parents for their children is more a love that comes down than a love that goes up. Parents of course live through great moments of joy in receiving the affection or recognition of their children, but they also must expect to give much more than they receive; this is their lot in life. They must not require recognition or gratitude because of what they've done for their children. It's a great thing when they receive it, but it must not be a requirement, and the majority of times this gratitude will not be proportional to what they have given or suffered through. They must accept that their love will often be misunderstood, sometimes even rejected or disdained. This is what the Father in heaven experienced with his own children. The servant is not above the master; the earthly father, as well as the spiritual one, must also expect and accept this. Your consolation will not always come from your children, but it will come from God, because he loves and suffers with you and like you.

Exercising fatherhood requires accepting the inevitable injustice that will ensue. There's a sacrificial dimension to fatherhood. If we don't consent to this, we will be deceiving ourselves and subjecting ourselves to bitterness and permanent resentment. We can't expect that our children will make us happy; it's too much to ask of them. Only God is capable of this.

Let's conclude our reflection on the beatitudes as a spiritual path that allows the blossoming of a true fatherhood. It's a demanding path, but in the end it's a liberating one, full of peace and fruitfulness.

13

The Church, Mary, and the Mystery of the Woman

In the natural order, just as a woman can't become a mother without a man, a man cannot become a father without a woman. There is no paternity without conjugality. It's a beautiful truth that God didn't want either sex to be self-sufficient, and that each needs the other to accomplish its own vocation. Today we are unfortunately in the midst of a lot of confusion in this domain, a domain that is one of the most beautiful parts of God's plan for man and woman.

There is a certain analogy here between this reality and the question of priestly paternity. We already remarked above how a priest cannot become a father without a deep link to the mystery of the Church, without being a spouse of the Church. The mediation of the Church is necessary for him to be able to engender children in the life of grace. Reciprocally, the existence of priestly ministry in the Church, without being the only ministry, of course, is one of the most important ways that the Church exercises its spiritual maternity, its mission to "[bring] forth to a new and immortal life the sons who are born to her in baptism, conceived of the Holy Spirit, and born of God," according to Vatican II's expression.[1]

The Virgin Mary, a perfect image of the Church and also spiritual mother to all believers, has a big role to play in priestly paternity. All the more, since she is the mother of the only true priest, Jesus Christ, from whom the Church derives all priesthood. We cannot fully be priests without welcoming Mary, as one might welcome a well-loved disciple (see Jn 19:25–27). We must receive her fully in the intimacy of our lives, like one of the most precious gifts that God can give us, as much for our Christian perfection as for the fruitfulness of our pastoral ministry.

As I've already said, we can't be the father of souls except by being a son of the Church. We must also be a son of Mary if we want our priesthood to have the fullness of fruitfulness, particularly in the domain of spiritual fatherhood. I spoke of Pope St. John Paul II as one of the most beautiful examples of paternity

---

1. Dogmatic Constitution on the Church *Lumen Gentium* (November 21, 1964), no. 64. Vatican website: *www.vatican.va*.

that I was ever privileged to encounter. I was persuaded that there was an intimate connection between this spiritual paternity and his profound love for the Virgin Mary.

In his letter to priests for Holy Thursday 1988, St. John Paul II reminds us of the beautiful truth of our faith concerning the mystery of the Church's spiritual motherhood in relation to the motherhood of the Virgin. He connects this reality with the spiritual fatherhood of the priest:

> On Holy Thursday, we need to deepen once again this mysterious truth of our vocation: this "spiritual fatherhood" which on the human level is similar to motherhood. Moreover, does not God himself, the Creator and Father, make the comparison between his love and the love of a human mother (cf. Is 49:15; 66:13)? Thus we are speaking of a characteristic of our priestly personality that expresses precisely apostolic maturity and spiritual "fruitfulness." If the whole Church "learns her own motherhood from Mary," do we not need to do so as well? Each of us, then, has to "take her to our own home" like the Apostle John on Golgotha, that is to say, each of us should allow Mary to dwell "within the home" of our sacramental priesthood, as mother and mediatrix

of that "great mystery" (cf. Eph 5:32) which we all wish to serve with our lives.[2]

We know how much the Marian spirituality of John Paul II was nourished by the writings of St. Louis de Montfort. It was in reading the *Treatise on True Devotion* while he worked during the war at the Solvay factory in Krakow that the future pope was freed from this fear that giving too much priority to Mary in his piety could turn him from the centrality of the mystery of Christ. He understood that the more Mary is present in our lives, the closer we get to Christ.[3]

---

2. Pope John Paul II, Letter of the Holy Father John Paul II to Priests for Holy Thursday 1988. Vatican website: *www.vatican.va*.

3. St. John Paul II wrote in a letter in 2000 that, thanks to St. Louis de Montfort, he understood that authentic devotion to the Mother of God is truly Christocentric. "For me, St. Louis Marie Grignion de Montfort is a significant person of reference who has enlightened me at important moments in life. When I was working as a clandestine seminarian at the Solvay factory in Krakow, my spiritual director advised me to meditate on the True Devotion to the Blessed Virgin. . . . By relating the Mother of Christ to the Trinitarian mystery, Montfort helped me to understand that the Virgin belongs to the plan of salvation, by the Father's will, as the Mother of the incarnate Word, who was conceived by her through the power of the Holy Spirit. Mary's every intervention in the work of the regeneration of the faithful is not in competition with Christ, but derives from him and is at his service. Mary's action in the plan of salvation is always Christocentric." John Paul II, Letter to the Participants in the 8th International Mariological Colloquium (October 13, 2000), Servants of the Pierced Hearts of Jesus and Mary, *https://piercedhearts.org/jpii/speeches/2000/oct_13_louis_montfort.htm*.

The essential intuition that weaves its way throughout Montfort's writings can be summed up by this: "[Mary] gives her whole self, and gives it in an unspeakable manner, to him who gives all to her," and "if a soul gives itself to her without reserve, she gives herself to that soul without reserve."[4]

If we consecrate ourselves entirely to her, she will make us a part of everything she received from God: her faith, her humility, her charity, her purity, and so on. There is a great, deep mystery here—hidden to sages and wise men but revealed to the littlest ones—a very beautiful and effective path to holiness, interior transformation, and fruitfulness.

Whatever manner our own expression of living this consecration to Mary may take—and there are many forms it can take—she is, it seems to me, a necessity for our priesthood. Let's not deprive ourselves of the spiritual motherhood of Mary, this extraordinary channel of grace that the Father instituted for his children through the words of his crucified Son: "Woman, behold, your son! . . . Behold your mother!" (Jn 19:26–27). Mary welcomes us fully as her children, even more so since

---

4. *True Devotion*, p. 152 and p. 190. [Translator's note: Quotations from: *http://www.catholicwaypublishing.com/wp-content/uploads/2018/03/True-Devotion-to-Mary-With-Preparation-Saint-Louis-de-Montfort-5x8-Paperback-PDF-Edition.pdf*, p. 95 and p. 116]

we participate in the priesthood of her son. Let us also fully welcome her in return as our true mother: the most merciful, the most tender, the most powerful of mothers. What an immense gift for our life and our ministry to know that Mary will do for us everything that the most attentive of mothers can do for their children. We should lack nothing! What trust and peace we should have!

I've mentioned above the importance of the spirit of faith in the ministry and life of a priest. I would like to quote a wonderful text by Louis de Montfort, in which he describes Mary's faith, which is the principal gift that she gives to those who are consecrated to her:

> Our Blessed Lady will give you also a portion of her faith, which was the greatest of all faiths that ever were on earth, greater than the faith of all the Patriarchs, Prophets, Apostles, and Saints put together. . . . a pure faith which will make you hardly care at all about the sensible and the extraordinary; a lively faith animated by charity, which will enable you to perform all your actions from the motive of pure love; a faith firm and immovable as a rock, through which you will rest quiet and constant in the midst of storms and hurricanes; a faith active and piercing, which, like a mysterious pass-key, will give you entrance into all the mysteries of Jesus, into

the Last Ends of man, and into the Heart of God Himself; a courageous faith, which will enable you to undertake and carry out without hesitation great things for God and for the salvation of souls; lastly, a faith which will be your blazing torch, your divine life, your hidden treasure of divine wisdom, and your omnipotent arm, which you will use to enlighten those who are in the darkness of the shadow of death, to inflame those who are lukewarm and who have need of the heated gold of charity, to give life to those who are dead in sin, to teach and overthrow, by your meek and powerful words, the hearts of marble and the cedars of Lebanon, and finally, to resist the devil and all the enemies of salvation.[5]

In the natural domain of relationships between man and woman, we know how a woman can help a man become a father, encouraging him to assume his fatherhood. It isn't always easy for a man to become a father; there can be a tendency to flee this responsibility for various reasons: a lack of self-confidence, a lack of courage or responsibility, a fear of the unknown involved in this

---

5. *Treatise on True Devotion to the Blessed Mother*, Éditions Média-spaul, p. 223. [Translator's note: Quotations from: *http://www.catholicway publishing.com/wp-content/uploads/2018/03/True-Devotion-to-Mary-With-Preparation-Saint-Louis-de-Montfort-5x8-Paperback-PDF-Edition. pdf*, p. 135–136]

little, new life that is placed in his arms. A woman's attitude can be very positive for giving him confidence and encouraging him to take up the role that he is called to. We also know that, unfortunately, the inverse can happen: a woman can very easily discourage the paternal role of her spouse. Sometimes we see this with particular couples. The woman, who is more intuitive, better perceives problems, feels more responsible in general than the man, and therefore can sometimes have a tendency to take charge of everything, not leaving her husband his rightful place as father.

A very sad thing happening in parts of our culture today is that man and woman become enemies of one another, starting a power struggle instead of mutually helping and loving each other, each one according to the grace received. A man can bear much responsibility for a lack of respect for women, for how he may subject or exploit them sometimes, but a woman can also have her share of fault, especially in not helping the man with his proper role and with his fatherhood.

In the life of a priest, it can happen that a woman (a mother, a sister, a collaborator, or a friend) has a positive role in revealing and encouraging our paternity. Through her righteous attitude, through her way of tending to her ministry, through her esteem, affection, or prayer, she can be a great gift. It's often a woman who asks a priest to exercise his ministry (in confession, advice, direction, and the like) and, in so doing, ignites in him the grace of fatherhood. A lot of priests would never have become the fathers they are if they had not, at one moment of life or another, had this holy feminine presence helping them. I am thinking, for example, of the discreet but important presence of Catherine Lassagne for the Curé of Ars!

These relationships must be regulated, which isn't always easy. A woman can be nothing other than a mother or a sister for a priest, as John Paul II reminds us,[6] but her presence can be very fertile. In the history of the Church, examples of such women are innumerable (consecrated women in particular)—women who exercised a spiritual maternity toward priests, introducing them into the fullness of their priesthood.

I would also add that, in return, priests have an important role in letting women better discover their place in the mystery and life of the Church and thus contribute to its mission with their own genius.

---

6. John Paul II, Letter to Priests for Holy Thursday 1995. Vatican website: *www.vatican.va*. The letter describes the place of women in the life of the priest and is a beautiful reflection on women as sisters.

14

Baptismal and Ministerial Priesthood

The priest should have a concern for the laity and their capacity to fully succeed in their essential role in the life and mission of the Church. He should be at the service of families, letting all laypersons, of whatever state, find their place, responsibility, and contribution to evangelization or to other missions of the Church.

The promotion of the laity's place (especially today) in the life of the Church and especially in announcing the gospel is something that priests should really have close at heart. There are many social milieus that priests don't have access to, where laypersons are present. Some responsibilities that priests have assumed could be shared with laypeople, giving priests more availability for what is essential to our mission: prayer, celebration of the sacraments, preaching the gospel, and so forth.

I also think that we haven't yet fully realized all the consequences of the Second Vatican Council, which

wanted to reprioritize the common priesthood of the
faithful.[1] In the end, the most widespread priesthood
in the Church is not the ministerial priesthood but
the common priesthood of the baptized. The ministerial priesthood of priests is at the service of the common priesthood of the baptized, and not the reverse.
Priests have an extremely important role in igniting
and encouraging the faithful in the accomplishment
of their baptismal priesthood. Remember the touch-
ing words of St. Peter, speaking to all the baptized
and continuing in the vein of the Old Testament that
spoke of Israel as a priestly people:[2] "Like living stones
be yourselves built into a spiritual house, to be a holy
priesthood, to offer spiritual sacrifices acceptable to
God through Jesus Christ" (1 Pt 2:5). Listen also to
St. Paul's words in the Letter to the Romans: "I appeal
to you therefore, brethren, by the mercies of God,
to present your bodies as a living sacrifice, holy and
acceptable to God, which is your spiritual worship"
(Rom 12:1).

One of the essential roles of the priest is, through
words, example, and attitude, to encourage all the

---

1. *Lumen Gentium*, no. 10.

2. "You shall be to me a kingdom of priests and a holy nation. These
are the words which you shall speak to the children of Israel" (Ex 19:6).

faithful to exercise their baptismal priesthood, whatever vocation they may have: giving God the worship of praise and thanksgiving, interceding for the whole world, offering themselves to the Father out of love, offering themselves to the world with its joys and pains, "consecrating" to him in a certain way the whole universe—without forgetting to preach the gospel and witness to charity.

In the priesthood there is the beautiful role of mediation between God and his people: introducing men to God and God to men. It's true for the priest, but also for each one of the faithful.

The priest has the sacred power of consecrating the bread and the wine to transform them into the Body and Blood of Christ, but in an analogous way, the laity, through their lives and prayers, can offer and consecrate the entire world to God. It seems to me that this magnificent reality, of which the Council reminds us, is still far from being fully ensconced in the mentality and life of the faithful.

In Judaism, the father of the family plays a very noble role in presiding over the different familial liturgies such as the beginning of Sabbath on Friday night and the Passover Seder meal. It seems to me that an analogous reality could be better lived in Christian families, favoring both the man's exercise of certain aspects of this common priesthood he is clothed with, and simultaneously expressing the grace of his fatherhood, by presiding over family prayer, blessing the table, sharing the gospel, blessing children, and similar activities.[3]

---

3. There are some interesting avenues for theological reflection on the connection between priesthood and paternity, including its relationship with the priesthood of the baptized and ministerial priesthood, in the spiritual experience of Sr. Mary of the Trinity, a little-known contemporary mystic. See, in the records of the colloquium held at Ars in 2019, *Priests, a question of paternity* (ed. Artège Lethielleux), organized by the John-Marie Vianney Society, the conference of Sr. Alexandra Diriart on the paternity of the priest in relation to female consecrated life, pp. 254–256.

PART THREE

A Tangible Reality

15

Fatherhood in the Priest's Ministry

Having spoken of the spiritual fatherhood of priests, I would like to consider the way that this fatherhood is lived and exercised in the various concrete aspects of their ministry. The life and ministry of the priest can take extremely different forms. There is no single model; each priest has his own specific way of exercising his ministry and living his fatherhood. Therefore, I don't intend to propose rules that automatically apply to all, but only give some thoughts.

Intercession for the People

It's obvious that the first duty of a priest, and the first expression of his fatherhood, is to pray for the people entrusted to him. Of all of the things that Scripture tells us about the priesthood, particularly Christ's priesthood, this role of intercession is fundamental. The numerous examples of intercession witness to this, as well as the exhortations to prayer that we find in the Gospels and other New Testament writings. We could mention several passages, such as the priestly prayer of Jesus in chapter 17 of John's Gospel, as well as the affirmations from the Letter to the Hebrews: "He holds his priesthood permanently, because he continues forever. Consequently he is able for all time to save those who draw near to God through him, since he always lives to make intercession for them" (Heb 7:24–25).

One of the fundamental dimensions of the priesthood, already present in the Old Testament but accomplished and entirely renewed in the mystery of Christ, is the offering of sacrifices for the people so that God will be merciful, an offering united in intercessory prayer. The priest offers the redeeming sacrifice of Jesus for the people, while also offering himself in sacrifice as he begs God for the people's needs. Offering and intercession are two realities that cannot be separated from each other. "To intercede is to give one's blood," some Greek fathers say. Without offerings or sacrifice, prayer has no weight. Without prayer, offerings don't rise toward God.

In intercession there is an authentic form of fatherhood: to pray for someone means to give him life. A priest friend of mine shared with me once that through interceding for a long time for a person who was suffering greatly, he began to gain consciousness of his own fatherhood.

The Bible gives us magnificent examples of intercession: the prayer of Abraham for Sodom and Gomorrah (see Gn 18:16–33) and the intercession of Moses to obtain pardon for the people after the golden calf episode, which I already mentioned (see Ex 32).

When the Curé of Ars arrived at the almost-dead parish that his bishop gave him, his first task was to engage deeply in prayer, supplication, and penitence. It was after this first phase that his charism as a confessor began to be manifested.

Prayer for the people is a demanding duty, but it's also a grace and a consolation: we can't meet with everybody, we can't make everybody come to Mass, we can't convince everybody—far from it. But we can always pray for everybody, beg on their behalf, and entrust them to God. We know that our prayer is fruitful, because God instituted us as intercessors for his people. When Jesus tells us that he no longer calls us servants but friends (Jn 15:15), he makes, I dare say, a bad deal: servants can be refused, but with friends it is impossible. So much more so as he adds: "You did not choose me but I chose you and appointed you that you should go and bear fruit and that your fruit should abide; so that whatever you ask the Father in my name, he may give it to you" (Jn 15:16).

We should seize on these words in faith, believing in the power of our prayer not by virtue of our merit or our dignity but because we are supported by the inexhaustible merit of Jesus, and because we have been established, by God himself, as intercessors for his people. We have been called to unite ourselves to the effective prayer of Jesus, the Great Priest, for the salvation of all humanity.

I love these words from Isaiah: "Upon your walls, O Jerusalem, I have set watchmen; all the day and all the night they shall never be silent. You who put the Lord in remembrance, take no rest, and give him no rest until he establishes Jerusalem and makes it a praise in the earth" (Is 62:6–7). God himself invites us not to give him repose so long as he has not had mercy on his people! Our prayer should be incessant, like that of the persistent widow. "And will not God vindicate his elect, who cry to him day and night?" (Lk 18:7).

One of the great architects of the priestly renewal in the seventeenth century in France, Jean-Jacques Olier, wrote a draft of a rule for seminarians. He was one of the first to put it in place, to remedy the deficient formation of priests as called for by the Council of Trent. He insists in this text on the importance of formation in prayer. Before being a place of theological or pastoral formation, the seminary must be above all a school for prayer. He makes a remark that could seem curious to us today:

According to St. Gregory [St. Gregory the Great, pope and spiritual writer from the sixth century] we must, before being a priest, have acquired such a familiarity with God that we can't be refused: such that he who is admitted to an interview with God and who has no experience of having the power to appease him when he's irritated, should not be a priest nor be admitted as a pastor in the Church, for whom one of the principal obligations, after that of his own salvation and love of neighbor, is to appease the anger of God and reconcile the world to him."[1]

I don't know if in today's seminaries we can take up this criterion for discernment in calling someone to the priesthood: having had the experience of being enough of a friend of God to appease his anger and obtain his favor for the people. In any case, there is here a wonderful reference to Moses and other great intercessor-friends of God from the Old Testament, and it's an intuition that seems true to me. In intercession we find a primordial role of the priest, and a privileged place for exercising paternity. Through his prayer, he can touch in an invisible but effective way all those he can't otherwise reach through his ministry.

---

1. Cited in Jean-Jacques Olier, *Vivre pour Dieu en Jésus Christ*. Texts collected by Michel Dupuy, Cerf. 1995. [Translator's note: Translation mine]

The Celebration of the Eucharist and the Sacraments

In the celebration of the Eucharist, it's clear that the priest exercises fatherhood. He gives the people entrusted to him the food that they need: The Word of Truth and the Bread of Life. In the Eucharist the ministry of intercession and offering that I mentioned above are lived in the most intense and rich way.

In distributing Communion, the priest has this deep joy of giving God himself—nothing is equal to this—as food for the faithful. I remember hearing an old, married, Anglican priest, who later became Catholic, tell me his joy: "I am now certain that what I have in my hands and that I give to the faithful is truly the Body and Blood of Christ!"

I would make one simple remark: in making the most beautiful and fertile offering that we can imagine for the people to the Father, that of his own Son given up for us, it is not just the body of Christ that he offers to the faithful, but his own Person. Writing to priests for Holy Thursday 2005, John Paul II said:

> Christ's self-giving, which has its origin in the Trinitarian life of the God who is Love, reaches its culmination in the sacrifice of the Cross, sacramentally anticipated in the Last Supper. It is impossible to

repeat the words of consecration without feeling oneself caught up in this spiritual movement. *In a certain sense, when he says the words: "take and eat," the priest must learn to apply them also to himself, and to speak them with truth and generosity.* If he is able to offer himself as a gift, placing himself at the disposal of the community and at the service of anyone in need, his life takes on its true meaning.[2]

On this subject I would like to quote the beautiful words of Cardinal Nguyen Van Thuan. He spent more than thirteen years in the communist prisons of Vietnam and found in the Eucharist the strength to live through this terrible period with an unfailing faith and boundless charity. Here is how he witnesses to the moments when he celebrated Mass and gave Communion secretly to other Catholic prisoners:

> I offer the Mass with the Lord: when I distribute Communion I give myself too with the Lord, making myself food for all. This means that I am always totally at the service of others. Each time that I offer Mass I have the opportunity to stretch out my hands and be nailed to the Cross with Jesus, to drink the

---

2. John Paul II, Letter of the Holy Father John Paul II to Priests for Holy Thursday 2005. Vatican website: *www.vatican.va*. Emphasis adapted.

bitter cup with him. Each day, in reciting or listening to the words of the consecration, I confirm with all my heart and all my soul a new pact, an eternal covenant between me and Jesus, through his Blood mixed with mine.[3]

For the priest, the celebration of the Mass is the highest and greatest aspect of his ministry. He was instituted as a priest primarily because of the Eucharist. The simple fact of saying Mass justifies his existence. It is both the source and the ultimate goal of his life. It is the source of his strength, his peace, his pastoral generosity, and his joy. It summarizes both the goal and meaning of all his life: offering himself like and with Jesus in sacrifice and praise for the glory of the Father and the salvation of all people.

Eucharistic Adoration

I've already spoken of the importance of Eucharistic Adoration in the life of the priest. This is where he unites himself to Christ, and where he receives from God the grace of his own fatherhood.

Paradoxically, adoration is the highest and most effective apostolical activity. The priest welcomes God

---

3. Quoted by Fr. François-Marie Léthel, "'*I Carry You with Me Day and Night*': The Eucharistic Spirituality of Cardinal Nguyen Van Thuan," Zenit (French), March 29, 2020. [Translator's note: Translation mine]

here, for himself and for all those who don't welcome him, and he lets himself be drawn in by him, with the certainty that in this way many other people will also be drawn toward his love. "And I, when I am lifted up from the earth, will draw all men to myself," Jesus says (Jn 12:32). We know Thérèse of Lisieux's wonderful intuition when she commented on the verse from the Song of Songs and its curious shift from the singular to the plural: "Draw me after you, let us make haste" (Song 1:4). She understood that, once a soul lets itself be attracted to God, it is never alone, but it drags others along who run by its side.[4]

Putting yourself in God's presence in the name of all the people the Lord has entrusted to you, in the silence of adoration, is a secret but real way of birthing them into the divine life.

I also recall the wonderful witness of John Paul II on his experience:

> It is pleasant to spend time with him, to lie close to his breast like the Beloved Disciple (cf. Jn 13:25), and to feel the infinite love present in his heart. If in our time Christians must be distinguished above all by the "art of prayer," how can we not feel a renewed

---

4. Ms C, 34r.

need to spend time in spiritual converse, in silent adoration, in heartfelt love before Christ present in the Most Holy Sacrament? How often, dear brothers and sisters, have I experienced this, and drawn from it strength, consolation and support![5]

Personal Dialogue

There's a great need among the faithful for listening and spiritual accompaniment. It isn't always easy for a priest to be available to those who manifest this desire, but he must be available as much as possible. While being very humble, prudent, and attentive to his own formation, he must have trust in the grace that rests on him in this domain.

These times of personal dialogue are a grace for the people who benefit from the priest's acceptance and attention, but they're also a grace for the priest himself. I have learned more in meeting and listening than I have in all of my studies. Here is where we see human reality in all its diversity, its complexity, its light, and its shadow; but we also notice in a beautiful way the work of divine grace, the movement of the Holy Spirit among people of good will who desire to let themselves be led by God, and who thus exhibit the humble attitude of

---

5. Pope John Paul II, Encyclical Letter on the Eucharist in Its Relationship to the Church *Ecclesia de Eucharistia* (April 17, 2003). Vatican website: *www.vatican.va*.

trust which is the basis of spiritual dialogue. Hearing someone tell you, as has happened to me several times, "Father, I want to share with you something I've never told anyone," and then noticing how this attitude of sincere openness can be beneficial and open one up to God's actions, is a rich experience.

This is one of the privileged places where the priest can exercise a fertile fatherhood, transmitting divine life, helping people become more fully themselves. It's a complex area, sometimes delicate, but I don't want to examine it at great length; instead, I will simply make a few remarks.

Even if the words "spiritual direction" make sense (they're part of the classical vocabulary of the Christian tradition, although today we prefer to speak of "accompaniment"), it's clear that it has nothing to do with "directing" people according to our own ideas by imposing on them whatever they may be, but instead helping them to perceive and follow the lead of the Holy Spirit. It requires all the qualities that I spoke of above: an unconditional and loving acceptance, an attentive listening, an immense respect for the person and their freedom, a total selflessness regarding one's own views and ideas so as to let God's wisdom act in them, a wisdom that is unique for each person and that can sometimes be unsettling.

The first benefit from spiritual dialogue for the person who asks for it is that it moves things from the subjective sphere, and sometimes confused emotions, to the objective sphere, that of language and dialogue. Expressing in terms comprehensible for another what we are living through on the inside is in itself very positive, because it permits us to distance ourselves from feelings in order to see them objectively. This alone can be pacifying and freeing, helps to de-dramatize the situation, puts things in perspective, and helps us see life in a more balanced way.

The second benefit is that the attitude of humility and trust that is linked to this sharing creates an opening for God's grace, for his light, and for his intervention in the life of the person. Sometimes this intervention is simple and discreet, sometimes more robust, according to what is appropriate in the given circumstance.

St. John of the Cross affirms that God wants people to need one another and wants them to let themselves be guided by each other, rather than clinging to their own judgment.[6] Modern individualism would do well to remember this: no one is self-sufficient and no one can find within himself all the light he needs. There is

---

6. *Ascent of Mount Carmel*, book II chapter 22. He gives the example of Moses, who saw God face-to-face, but who still needed the advice of his father-in-law, Jethro (Ex 18:14–23).

a "blessing" by the Father that rests on the spiritual dialogue. What's at play here is not merely human wisdom or a psychological experience, but the true work of the presence and action of God. "Where two or three are gathered in my name, there am I in the midst of them," Jesus affirms (Mt 18:20).

This grace, this visit from God, is accomplished through the sincerity of the accompanying person's approach, the welcoming quality of listening (people must feel loved as they are, including in what they are living through), and through communal prayer. It is also accomplished through the advice that can be given, the words that the accompanying person perceives must be communicated. It is important therefore to listen to the person deeply before giving advice. We must not be too hasty to give advice or to furnish solutions; we must avoid giving ready-made recipes or moralizing advice that doesn't respond to another's suffering. When advice is given, we must also verify how it is received and understood, determining whether it is a source of peace and encouragement. We must sometimes accept the poverty of not having much to say. We must not see ourselves as obliged to have an immediate response to all the questions and a solution to all the problems, but always remain very humble. Don't say or do more than the grace that is given.

Listening to people and praying with them is already an enormous thing.

Spiritual accompaniment and listening are not reserved just for priests, of course; laypersons can also practice these. And not all priests have the same grace for this, either. But it's good when they make themselves available for this as much as possible. It amounts to being available, and it's an important place for watchfulness and for exercising fatherhood—so much more so when the priest has the chance to combine spiritual accompaniment with the grace of confession.

Finally, let's remember that the priest himself needs to be accompanied. No one will find all the light he needs for his path within himself alone. Even the greatest saints felt a great need to open their soul to someone else.

Confession

What a shame it is that so many Christians deprive themselves of confession, and that some priests don't encourage them more to make regular use of it. For the faithful, the sacrament of reconciliation is a unique occasion to experience the merciful fatherhood of God. It allows us to encounter God not as a judge who accuses, but as a father who welcomes, pardons, and heals.

For the priest, it's a great gift to be a witness and an instrument of divine mercy, and to observe the marvel of what God's love can accomplish in the hearts of his people. What peace, what spiritual joy and interior healing are given during this sacrament.

Obviously, this outcome requires on the penitent's side that the confession not be something formal, but that it express a true repentance, a real desire for conversion and for progress in a life according to the gospel, as well as great trust in God.

On his side, the priest must be conscious of the immense grace that is conveyed by pronouncing the words of absolution that pour forth the power and authority of the Divine Word himself. He should be amazed that God has "given such authority to men," as the crowds said after Jesus assured the paralytic that his sins were forgiven and healed him (Mt 9:8). This ought to inspire in the priest a great awe of God, that he has received such a ministry in spite of his unworthiness.

It's an occasion for the confessor to practice the paternal attitude that we already mentioned: welcoming people with generosity, so that they may feel loved just as they are and not judged. The priest must not be surprised at anything; even the worst faults should not inspire a feeling of revulsion or disdain. His task is not to add to the reproaches that penitents already feel, making the weight of shame still heavier; it is rather to assure them of God's mercy. Who am I after all to judge others? I could have done worse if God hadn't spared me!

The confessor should not show any curiosity beyond what people confide in him (even if he has the right sometimes to ask certain questions with the sole goal of better helping the penitent), and should have much respect and delicacy, like a good doctor faced with a fragile sick person. He must help the other to convert and to grow according to the gospel, seeing more clearly perhaps the reality of his sin and the conversion that is demanded of him, but without imposing something that would be beyond the penitent's strength. As much as possible, the person should leave the confessional peaceful and consoled, certain of having advanced in sanctity and counting on the love of God.

It's clear that the priest will be a good confessor only if he himself frequently goes to confession. In France in the 1970s, I knew priests who were not very inclined to listen to people in confession and who preferred to be content with collective absolutions, because they themselves didn't go to confession. Those times have happily passed.

Preaching

The ministry of preaching during Mass, as well as other occasions to teach the faithful, is also an extremely important part of spiritual fatherhood. Like a father who provides food for his children, the priest who preaches or teaches communicates the truth that makes us free, and gives the Word of Life to the faithful. This is a vast area of the pastoral ministry, a subject on which I will content myself to make only a few remarks.

For our preaching to be fertile, to touch the hearts of listeners and nourish them, it must be simple, direct, Scripture-based, and founded in prayer. It's not about making grand discourses but instead deploying the infinite riches of the Word of God for the faithful. It's about permitting the faithful to experience what St. Paul said: "For whatever was written in former days was written for our instruction, that by steadfastness and by the encouragement of the scriptures we might have hope" (Rom 15:4).

We must avoid going off on tangents unrelated to the Mass readings. Sometimes this happens as a necessity, but usually we must take up the biblical readings to make the light and nourishment that God has put in them available to his people, and to make the message of the gospel current and applicable in their concrete lives.

We can't touch souls unless we ourselves have been touched. This requires that before preaching, we have taken a good amount of time to pray, invoking the Holy Spirit to open our minds to understand the Scriptures (see Lk 24:45), meditating on the biblical passages on which we are called to preach, and letting them profoundly resonate in our own hearts, so as to transmit them later to the faithful. More than intellectual reflection, or a search for new or original ideas, or brilliant study, prayer is the secret of preaching. Through prayer, we let ourselves be instructed by God who speaks to our hearts and can also instruct others.

Always remember that when we meditate on Scripture, it is not above all to convert others, but to convert ourselves. Don't forget that this is the secret of exegesis: the sincere desire for conversion. What makes Scripture open its hidden treasures is not knowledge (even if a good biblical formation is necessary), but rather a great desire for conversion when approaching the Divine Word. We ask God that it be for us, as the author of the Letter to the Hebrews said, a living and active word, "sharper than any two-edged sword, piercing to the division of soul and spirit, of joints and marrow, and discerning the thoughts and intentions of the heart" (Heb 4:12).

Preaching is sometimes a place for combat: we can feel dry, lacking, not knowing what to say—or even have the feeling that our homily is really lame. It's a great pleasure to preach when the grace is there, when God clearly inspires us with what to say, more precisely than if we read from a text. Sometimes it humiliates us when we seem to bore our listeners. We must consent to this without getting discouraged. We must live this ministry with a lot of humility, sometimes accepting a certain poverty, not trying to be brilliant or original, but simply saying what we have in our hearts to our listeners and having trust in God. If our desire is to sincerely communicate the light and love of God to the faithful through our language, being simple servants of the Word and without seeking personal success, even if the preaching is poor, God will know how to arrange things. We know that the Curé of Ars tried for years to laboriously prepare his sermons, before he settled on the simple, spontaneous, profound manner that so touched the hearts of his listeners.

The Government of a Community

A priest can be led in his ministry to receive the charge of governing a community: a diocese, a parish, a religious community, a movement, or any other ecclesial reality. This can also be a wonderful occasion for him to develop the grace of fatherhood. Examples abound from Church history of holy bishops, priests, pastors, and abbots.

This responsibility can sometimes be a heavy one (I mentioned Moses' complaints on this subject above!), as it demands a lot of devotion and energy. However, it can lead to great human and spiritual growth—no longer living for ourselves but for others, making concern for others surpass our own interests, realizing what is unique in each person, exercising patience and understanding, looking after the unity and spiritual vitality of the community, being in dialogue with all, and trusting in the Lord when difficult situations or decisions come up.

I was responsible for a community in Rome for thirteen years. It was not easy for me. I don't have any particular grace for governing, I don't have the vocation of "leading," and I am very happy not to have this responsibility any longer. That being said, I must recognize that it was a precious opportunity for purification, for progress, and for human and spiritual discovery that were certainly beneficial for my priesthood.

In the life of the Church, we sometimes confuse the grace of priesthood with the power of government, and I think that we would do well to distinguish them better, avoiding all forms of clericalism and abuse of authority, which have such sorrowful consequences. That being said, government of a community for a priest can be a very precious service and an authentic form of fatherhood. It obviously requires that the exercise of authority be lived in the spirit described in the course of this book: a fatherhood that is a service, a pure and disinterested love, to help others grow and not to make them subject to our will.

It also requires right perception when it comes to the spiritual dimension of authority in the Church. We notice this for example in Peter's beautiful words addressed to the elders in his first letter:

> So I exhort the elders among you, as a fellow elder and a witness of the sufferings of Christ as well as a partaker in the glory that is to be revealed. Tend the flock of God that is your charge, not by constraint but willingly, not for shameful gain but eagerly, not as domineering over those in your charge but being examples to the flock. (1 Pt 5:1–3)

It's striking to notice that in this passage Peter doesn't define the elders' role in terms of their social function but through a double spiritual experience: being *witnesses to the sufferings of Christ* and *sharing in the glory to be revealed*. The elder is not foremost a person who exercises such and such a responsibility, but is above all someone who understands Christ's sufferings, who has perceived the mercy and infinite love of God witnessed in the Passion, and who understands the beauty of the kingdom to come, the splendor of the hope that we have in Christ. Everything is referred back to the mystery of Christ.

The exercise of authority must then be lived in a just way, both spiritually and humanly, attentive in leading all toward their freedom as children of God. It must also be exercised in conformity with what the Church demands: in communion with other leaders, in submission to a superior authority, in respect of the instances when personal authority is limited or constrained (the councils of various bodies, dialogue, respect for norms and statutes, and so on). No one is above the law, which is there not to impose heavy rules but to protect the little ones.

We may criticize abuses of authority, and this can even be necessary. But it should not lead us to forget that exercising authority remains a precious and even indispensable service in the life of society and of the Church. Suppose that one day no one could exercise authority or be in a position to make courageous decisions, even unpopular ones, although necessary and legitimate—it would be a disaster for any society.

We must not forget, either, to do as the Scriptures invite us (see 1 Tm 2:1–2), to pray for those who direct us, for their task is often very difficult and thankless. We must also respect those who have the courage to accept these responsibilities, and try to facilitate their work rather than assail them with criticism.

Defending the Poor and the Little Ones

One aspect of priestly fatherhood, which ancient and recent Church history illuminates, is the defense of the poor and the powerless. For this, priests or bishops have paid with their lives. The list is very long, and examples can be found in all places and at all times.

A man who has a fatherly heart will have a particular tenderness for the most fragile, the poorest, the most injured of his children. It must be the same for a priest. His heart should be inhabited by this compassionate tenderness of God for the poor and the humble, which is so present in the Scriptures, as much in the Old Testament (often expressed in the Psalms, for example, and also evident in the confrontation between Elijah and Ahab over Naboth's vineyard [1 Kings 21]) as in Jesus' attitude depicted in the writings of the New Testament.

We see Jesus take up the defense of his disciples when criticized by the doctors of the law; the sinful woman who anoints his feet and who is judged by Simon the Pharisee; the children who run up to him; the little people disdained by the Sadducees or the scribes; and the poor widow who has only two small coins to put in the temple treasury.

Any time that a poor person is disdained, exploited, or humiliated in any way, a priest's heart should leap inside of him.

I don't want to say more on this subject, but I think that every priest should ask himself the question: who are the poor ones that God has entrusted to me particularly today in my ministry? The response can of course be extremely diverse according to each situation: lost young people, lonely or aged people, psychologically ill people, homeless people on the street, hearts that are wounded by a lack of love, people who are in great need of understanding or counsel, and many others. It's clear that if I am a parish priest, the first among them should be the parishioners that God has entrusted to me; if I am a preacher the first among them should be the people who have great need of the truth or encouragement that the gospel gives. But it seems to me that we should, as priests, have a clear understanding that we are servants of a certain category of poor people that Jesus entrusts to us in a special way.

It's inspiring to remember Jesus' words during the anointing at Bethany: "The poor you always have with you, but you do not always have me" (Jn 12:8).

Conclusion

❧

M any other things could be said on priestly father-hood. I have shared some reflections from my own experience, which is certainly a limited one. These reflections merit being completed, even corrected or improved on several points. My only goal is to encourage my brother priests in their great, beautiful ministry, and to invite the faithful to do the same. Remember Paul's edifying words in the Second Letter to the Corinthians: "Therefore, having this ministry by the mercy of God, we do not lose heart" (2 Cor 4:1).

The sorrowful failures that may exist in this domain, or the need to reform certain things in the Church, should not cause us to forget how rich and precious is the gift that the Lord made to the Church and to society as a whole through the priesthood. In living their priesthood with great humility and a constant effort at conversion and purification, priests should have full confidence in the grace that rests on them and believe in the blessing that they can be to God's people. The gift that was made to them must also be welcomed with gratitude by the faithful.

We must also recognize that their situation is not easy today. Their load is often very heavy, and they are sometimes very alone. They are occasionally the object of attacks that are harsh yet contradictory. For example, we ask them to live their role, being active and dynamic, but at the same time we don't want them to take on too many responsibilities and we suspect them of "clericalism." We want both open, accessible men, men just like other men, while we want them to be angels with no defects! They are sometimes the object of mistrust, and know that any error in their lives will be quickly spread by the media. The constraints that weigh on the lives of priests today are enormous, and they merit more consideration and mercy.

That being said, we must not let the problems of the priesthood, even if they are real and must be confronted courageously, lead us to a pessimism, a discouragement, a suspicion toward the Church. This would be to play into the hands of the enemy, who is always seeking to pillage the Church's treasures and to deprive it of its most precious possessions, especially joy and hope. In spite of the difficult context, priests must be happy to have been called to this ministry, to this participation in the priesthood of Jesus, which is a veritable gift for them and for the whole world. It's also necessary that the faithful be happy that they can benefit from the gift that the Holy Spirit has made to them thanks to the existence of the ministerial priesthood, being cognizant of it and grateful for it.

I would like my little work here to be a call for the intercession of the faithful for priests, for priestly vocations, and for this ministry of priests to be more than ever carried out with love, esteem, and prayer for all.

The vitality and holiness of the priesthood does not rest only on priests and the ecclesial institution. It is also the business of all the faithful. It is in the measure with which the people of God let themselves be always converted and renewed by the Holy Spirit that the priesthood also will be regenerated.

If we pray that the Lord give us holy priests, if families desire that God choose from among their children his future ministers, if we all do what is possible to surround them, sustain them, and love them, avoiding putting them on a pedestal or idealizing them, God will renew and purify the priesthood, giving the Church priests who will be torches of his light, his holiness, and his mercy, helping each one of the faithful to exercise in splendor their own baptismal priesthood in joy and freedom as children of God.

To finish, I leave you with the words of St. Paul:

> Such is the confidence that we have through Christ toward God. Not that we are sufficient of ourselves

to claim anything as coming from us; our sufficiency is from God, who has qualified us to be ministers of a new covenant, not in a written code but in the Spirit; for the written code kills, but the Spirit gives life.

Now if the dispensation of death, carved in letters on stone, came with such splendor that the Israelites could not look at Moses' face because of its brightness, fading as this was, will not the dispensation of the Spirit be attended with greater splendor? (2 Cor 3:4–8).

Completed on the Feast of the Curé of Ars,
August 4, 2020.